GCSE
Physical Education

Complete Revision and Practice

Contents

Section Four —
Training And Sporting Skills

Section Five — Sport in Society

Published by Coordination Group Publications Ltd

Contributors:
Emma Cannell, Charley Darbishire, Mary Falkner, Dee Gannon, Sandy Gardner,
David Hickinson, Simon Little, Adam Moorhouse, Andy Park, Glenn Rogers, Caley
Simpson, Sarah Williams.

With thanks to Chris Cope, Paul Jordin and Sharon Keeley for the proofreading.

Definition of Health on page 1 © WHO 2008. All rights reserved. World Health Organisation
http://www.who.int/about/definition/en/print.html

With thanks to the International Olympic Committee for use of the image on page 111.

ISBN: 978 1 84762 405 5

Website: www.cgpbooks.co.uk

Printed by Elanders Ltd, Newcastle upon Tyne.
Clipart source: CorelDRAW® and VECTOR

Based on the classic CGP style created by Richard Parsons.

PE and Your Healthy, Active Lifestyle

Competence, performance, creativity and health spring up everywhere in GCSE PE. You need to make sure you understand what each one means, and why it's important...

You Need to be **Competent** and **Creative** to **Perform Well**

1) You need to be competent to be able to do something successfully.

> **COMPETENCE** is the relationship between skill, and knowing how and when to use skills, tactics, strategies and compositional ideas. To be competent you need to be physically and mentally ready to do an activity.

So in rugby, being competent could mean using tactics like set plays. In dance, you need to know what ideas or emotions you're trying to get across through your movements.

2) To perform well you need to use your competencies.

> **PERFORMANCE** is using your physical competencies with your knowledge of a physical activity to produce an effective and successful result.

- In team sports, you need to use other people's strengths to help the team perform at its best — if someone's a great forward in football, it'd be silly to have them playing as a goalkeeper.
- To perform well, you need to know what counts as a success in an activity (e.g. scoring a goal) — otherwise you'll have no idea what you should be aiming to do.
- To perform better, you need to be able to analyse and evaluate your performance to see where you could improve.

3) Being creative can have huge advantages in all sorts of activities.

> **CREATIVITY** is where you explore and experiment with techniques, tactics and compositional ideas to produce successful results.

- Sometimes it's obvious when creativity is important, like in expressing and communicating ideas when choreographing a dance.
- Being creative also helps you try out different techniques and solve problems. Creative tactics are often the key to performing well.

PE can Help you Lead a **Healthy, Active Lifestyle**

1) Most of us exercise just to stay fit and healthy, or just for fun.
2) Being healthy is more than just having a healthy body. Remember this definition of health — it's the one used by the World Health Organisation (WHO).

> **Health** is a state of complete mental, physical and social well-being, and not just the absence of disease and infirmity.

PHYSICAL WELL-BEING:

1) Your heart, kidneys, and the rest of your body are working well.
2) You're not suffering from any diseases or injuries.
3) You're not physically weak (infirm), so you can easily do everyday activities.

MENTAL WELL-BEING:

1) You don't have too much stress or anxiety.
2) You're not suffering from any mental illnesses.
3) You feel content.

SOCIAL WELL-BEING:

1) You have food, clothing and shelter.
2) You have friends.
3) You believe you have some worth in society.

Healthy, Active Lifestyles

So, leading a <u>healthy</u>, <u>active lifestyle</u> isn't just about moving from in front of the TV once in a while (but that sure can help)... almost <u>everything</u> you do can affect your health.

Stay *Healthy* by Leading a *Healthy, Active Lifestyle*

1) Your <u>lifestyle</u> is the <u>way</u> you live your life. It's <u>everything</u> you do — including your <u>work</u> and <u>hobbies</u>.

> A **healthy, active lifestyle** adds to your <u>physical</u>, <u>mental</u> and <u>social well-being</u>. It includes <u>doing exercise</u> and <u>physical activity on a regular basis</u>.

2) For a healthy, active lifestyle — <u>exercise</u> and think <u>PEASED</u>.

P → <u>PERSONAL HYGIENE</u>:   Keep yourself <u>clean</u> — it'll help you to avoid loads of diseases. It won't do your <u>social</u> life any harm, either.

E → <u>EMOTIONAL HEALTH</u>:   Feeling good is important. Try to avoid too much <u>stress</u> and <u>worry</u>. This can be caused by <u>friends</u> and <u>relationships</u> as well as things like <u>work</u>.

A → <u>ALCOHOL / DRUG USE</u>:   Misuse of <u>substances</u> can lead to poor health. That includes <u>alcohol</u> and <u>tobacco</u>. Even breathing in other people's smoke (<u>passive smoking</u>) can lead to health problems.

S → <u>SAFETY</u>:   If you have a dangerous job or hobby, you're more likely to <u>injure</u> yourself. So use the proper <u>safety equipment</u> — and in sport, play by the rules.

E → <u>ENVIRONMENT</u>:   <u>Pollution</u> can cause <u>respiratory</u> problems. Noise can cause stress and affect your <u>sleep</u>. Studies have also shown the more access you have to <u>green space</u> like <u>parks</u> and <u>gardens</u>, the <u>better</u> your <u>mental well-being</u> is likely to be.

D → <u>DIET</u>:   You need the right balance of <u>nutrients</u> so you can cope with your lifestyle (see p45-46).

3) Your <u>job</u> can have a big effect — <u>manual</u> jobs and ones where you have to be <u>on your feet all day</u> are more <u>physically demanding</u> than office jobs. Similarly, jobs based <u>outdoors</u> are usually more physically demanding than those indoors. Working outdoors rather than cooped up in an office can be good for your <u>mental well-being</u> too. Getting a <u>physically active job</u> will contribute towards a healthy, active lifestyle.

There are ways to Measure *Health* and *Well-Being*

You've probably got a <u>good</u> general state of <u>health</u> and <u>well-being</u> if:

1) You're <u>satisfied</u> and happy with the different <u>parts</u> of your <u>life</u> (work, home etc.).

2) You have <u>positive feelings</u> more often than <u>negative</u> ones i.e. you're happy most of the time. This is a sign of having <u>good mental health</u>.

3) You've got plenty of <u>access to green space</u> — the more access you have, the more likely you are to be healthy. (Not only are you more likely to have a place to do physical activity, but being outdoors is good for you mentally too).

4) You do a <u>range of activities</u> — the happier and healthier you are, the more likely it is you'll want to <u>join in</u> different activities.

Healthy, Active Lifestyles

Doing exercise and physical activity is good for you — that's not exactly a surprise. What is surprising is just how many different ways it's good for you. Read and learn...

Physical Activity — Any Form of Exercise or Movement

1) Physical activity is just any form of exercise or movement. It can be planned and structured (like doing an aerobics class), or not (like dashing for the bus). In PE, you're normally interested in the structured and planned type.

> **Exercise** is any physical activity you do to improve or maintain your health and/or fitness.

It doesn't have to be a competitive sport.

2) To stay healthy, you need to be physically active. You can increase the amount of physical activity you do by just changing a few habits — like walking or cycling to school instead of getting the bus.

Physical Activity has Social, Physical and Mental Benefits

There's almost no end of good reasons for taking part in regular physical activity.

Social Benefits

1) FRIENDS — Doing physical activity can help you make friends with people of different ages and backgrounds. It might also just be a way of socialising with your current friends.

2) COOPERATION and TEAMWORK — By taking part in team activities like football, you have to learn how to cooperate and work with other people.

Physical Benefits

1) HEALTH — You can maintain or improve your health with regular physical activity. You reduce your chances of getting ill, and can increase your life expectancy.

2) FITNESS — You can increase or maintain your strength, endurance, flexibility and overall fitness (see p28).

3) PERFORMANCE — The more you do an activity, the better you'll get at it.

Mental Benefits

1) FEEL GOOD — As you do physical activity, your body releases more of a hormone called serotonin into your blood stream. Serotonin makes you feel happy — the higher your serotonin levels, the happier you feel.

2) STRESS RELIEF — Doing physical activity can help relieve stress and prevent stress-related illnesses.

3) SELF-ESTEEM — Taking part in a physical activity can improve your self-image, self-esteem, confidence, and generally make you feel better about yourself.

4) COMPETITION and PHYSICAL CHALLENGE — Whether you're in a competition, or just trying to better your last performance — physical activity can challenge you and drive you to do the best you can. It can also improve how you think and act under pressure.

5) ENJOYMENT — You might choose to do a certain activity because you enjoy it, whether you find it exciting or relaxing or somewhere in between.

Aesthetic Appreciation — How Good an Activity Looks

If you do an activity, you get a better understanding of it and the techniques involved. You also know what to watch out for, whether it's a great pass in football, or a punch combination in boxing. Having done the physical activity, you'll probably appreciate it more than someone who hasn't.

So P.E. is great for relieving stress — oh, apart from the exam...

Now that's a lot of benefits — make you know whether each benefit is social, mental or physical.

Roles in Sport

An <u>active participant</u> is anyone who takes part in a sport — but that doesn't just mean a player, oh no. There are loads of <u>different roles</u> in sport to take your pick from — and they all need <u>different skills</u>. <u>Improving</u> each set of skills is the main <u>benefit</u> of doing each role.

Players Perform and Organisers, well, Organise...

PLAYER/PERFORMER — someone who plays a sport or performs an activity

1) You normally become a player or performer because you <u>enjoy</u> doing a particular activity.
2) You get to have <u>fun</u>, and by <u>doing well</u> in the activity you get to <u>feel good</u> about yourself. You can also develop skills to <u>improve your performance</u>.
3) You need to be able to <u>listen</u> and <u>respond</u> to what your coach or team captain says, be able to <u>cooperate</u> and work with your <u>team</u>, and abide by the activity's <u>rules</u>.
4) You also need to be able to <u>adapt</u> to situations e.g. needing to change tactics during a tennis match.

ORGANISER — a player or non-player who brings together everything you need, when you need it

1) Organisers <u>arrange</u> and <u>coordinate</u> competitions and events, and organise <u>people</u> (players, officials, volunteers, etc.), <u>facilities</u> (e.g. booking pitches for practice sessions) and <u>time</u>. Being an organiser can also involve <u>supervising</u> other people, and <u>delegating</u> tasks (giving them out to other people).
2) A good organiser will show <u>initiative</u> and have a fine eye for <u>detail</u>. They can do wonders for <u>promoting</u> an <u>event</u>, <u>team</u> or <u>performance</u> — leading to <u>more people</u> coming to <u>watch</u> or <u>take part</u>.
3) By getting the <u>right people</u> in (e.g. top dancers) they can make sure they put on the best performance.
4) Being an organiser is a great way to stay involved in sport if you <u>can't participate</u> (e.g. through injury).

A Choreographer is the Designer of a Performance

<u>Choreographers design</u> and <u>arrange</u> staged performances — e.g. ballet.

1) Choreography is all about letting your <u>creative juices</u> flow by finding ways to <u>express an idea</u>.
2) A good choreographer can provide <u>exciting ideas</u> for dancers to work with.
3) Choreographers also have to <u>evaluate</u> dancer performance, and <u>communicate</u> with and <u>advise</u> performers on how to <u>improve</u> their individual and group performances.

All Sports need Officials

1) <u>Referees</u>, <u>officials</u> and <u>umpires</u> are the people who <u>control</u> what's going on in an activity.
2) They need to <u>know the rules</u> of their sport inside out, and have to be <u>observant</u> and <u>decisive</u> (as they often need to make decisions <u>quickly</u>).
3) They need to be <u>authoritative</u> and <u>confident</u> so they can keep <u>control</u> of the game. Once they've made a decision they need to be confident enough to <u>enforce</u> it even if players try to argue.
4) They're also responsible for checking the <u>equipment</u>.

By officiating, you can <u>improve</u> your knowledge of the <u>rules</u> of a game.
It's also another role that lets you <u>take part</u> in an activity when you're <u>unable to play</u>.

Make sure you know your organisers from your officials...

There are plenty of ways to be an active participant in sport, you can be a player (who plays — duh), an organiser, a choreographer or an official. There are even more roles coming up on the next page.

Roles in Sport

Once you've got some players, you're going to need someone to train and lead them...

Coaches and Team Captains Need to be Leaders

To be a good team captain or coach, you need to be able to lead and influence a group.
You also need to be enthusiastic about your sport and able to motivate yourself and your team.

COACH — a non-player that's in charge of training a group or individual

1) Coaches need to be specialists in their sport so they can come up with training ideas and game-winning tactics. They're often ex-players or ex-performers who want to stay involved in their activity.

2) They need to keep up with changing trends in the game, e.g. new styles of play in football, and adapt their training accordingly to help players improve, both individually and as a team.

3) They're responsible for making sure performers/players:
- are in the correct mental state — when learning new skills and during a performance.
- are in the correct physical state — that not only are they fit to perform (e.g. not injured), but they're in peak physical shape to perform at their best.
- have the correct techniques and skills they need to perform well.
- behave themselves and follow the rules within their sport or activity.

4) To help players and performers improve, they need to be able to set goals and monitor and evaluate performance. They also need to be able to communicate their advice clearly, both verbally and non-verbally (see p80), as well as listen and respond to the players.

CAPTAIN — a player that leads their team during a game

1) They should be highly skilled in their sport, and able to perform reliably under pressure. That way they can act as role models for the other members of their team.

2) They need to be decisive and adapt to situations during a game. E.g. cricket team captains have to decide how to arrange the fielders, and work out bowling tactics to try and beat the opposing team.

Captains also need to be organised — they're often responsible for arranging practice sessions and matches.

Volunteering — More Than a Nice Thing to Do

1) Being a volunteer means giving up your free time to do something without being paid. Sports volunteers can do anything from coaching, to driving the team minibus to matches, to washing the netball bibs.

2) Volunteers are really important in sport. Many sports clubs and initiatives are run by volunteers alone.

3) Volunteers need to be enthusiastic and able to work well as part of a team. Having leadership and problem-solving skills is always a bonus.

4) Yes, you have to work for free — but people usually get a lot back from volunteering. Helping people get into sport can be really satisfying. You can also make new friends, and improve your teamwork and leadership skills which are useful outside of sport.

5) It can also give you contacts which are really useful for getting more involved in sport. And the experience can make you generally more employable, too.

If only all coaches came with a TV, DVD player and air con...

There are lots of different roles an active participant can do. Make sure you know the qualities you need to be good at these different roles, as well as the reasons for doing them, and their benefits.

Choosing a Physical Activity

There are <u>loads</u> of different physical activities to chose from — and they all need different <u>skills</u>. Improving skills is one of the <u>benefits</u> of sport — if there's one specific skill you want to develop, you might choose a sport for that <u>reason</u>. You need to know the following types of activities, the <u>skills</u> you need to do them, and what counts as a <u>success</u> in each one. If you're <u>not</u> doing an AQA course, you can just skip this page.

*Different **Types of Activity** Require **Different Skills**...*

Games Activities

Games (in PE... not the board or card sort) are any physical activities where you play against <u>other people</u> using a <u>set of rules</u>. E.g. football, rounders, cricket, basketball, badminton, squash...

SKILL: To perform well and win games activities, you need to be able to <u>outwit</u> and <u>beat</u> your <u>opponents</u>. E.g. changing the <u>speed</u> and <u>spin</u> of a cricket ball to bowl a batsman out.

SUCCESS: Success is <u>beating your opponents</u> in competition by <u>affecting their performance</u>. E.g. <u>defending</u> well in football so the opponents are <u>unable to score</u>.

Athletic Activities

In athletics activities (e.g. high jump, 100 m sprint, archery...), you're judged on your <u>performance</u> in a particular activity. You can be either competing <u>directly</u> with other people, or with your previous <u>best</u> performance.

SKILL: In athletic activities, you might need jump the <u>furthest</u>, run the <u>fastest</u>, be the <u>strongest</u>, be the most <u>accurate</u>... you get the idea.

SUCCESS: Success in athletics can mean <u>beating</u> your <u>personal best</u> time, distance or score. If you're competing, you'll win if you get a better time or score than everyone else.

Dance Activities

There are loads of different types of dance activity (e.g. ballet, contemporary, folk...).

SKILL: Usually to dance well, you need to be able to <u>communicate</u> particular <u>ideas</u> or <u>emotions</u> through your <u>body movement</u>. You need to get any <u>technical dance steps</u> right too.

SUCCESS: Success is being able to <u>get across</u> whatever ideas or feelings you or the <u>choreographer</u> intended to get across to an <u>audience</u>.

Gymnastic Activities

SKILL: In gymnastics, it's really important to be able to <u>accurately copy</u> actions and <u>body movement sequences</u>.

SUCCESS: Success in gymnastics is being able to <u>repeat</u> these movements as <u>perfectly</u> as possible. This could be in anything from a series of somersaults in a floor routine, to the correct movement on the rings.

Survival and Adventure Activities

SKILL: You need to be able to <u>identify</u> and <u>solve</u> problems to overcome challenges, e.g. finding hand holds in rock climbing.

SUCCESS: Success is managing to get over the challenges <u>healthily</u> and <u>safely</u> (and, obviously, surviving...).

Fitness and Health Activities

Fitness and health activities are activities that improve your health and fitness, e.g. aerobics.

SKILL: The skill in these activities is just to be able to <u>safely</u> and <u>effectively</u> exercise to <u>improve</u> your health.

SUCCESS: Improved <u>fitness</u>, <u>health</u> and <u>wellbeing</u>.

Warm-Up and Worked Exam Questions

Warm-Up Questions

1) What is 'health'?
2) What is competence the relationship between?
3) What does PEASED stand for?
4) Describe the difference between physical activity and exercise.
5) Name three different roles active participants can have in sport.
6) What are the main responsibilities of an organiser?
7) Describe the qualities that are needed to be a good coach.
8) Describe the benefits people can get from volunteering in sport.

Worked Exam Questions

You will almost certainly get asked questions on healthy active lifestyles and roles in sport.
Make sure you can follow these worked examples, then have a go at the questions on the next page.

1   Jeff plays badminton three times a week at his local sports centre.
     Suggest **two** reasons why Jeff participates in physical activity.
     State whether each reason is social, physical or mental.

     Reason 1: *To relieve stress — a mental reason.*

     Reason 2: *To make friends — a social reason.*

     There are loads of different reasons for doing physical activity (see page 3), but you only need to put down two to get the marks.

     (4 marks)

2   What is meant by the term 'performance'? Give **one** example of what might count
     as success for a performer in a named physical activity.

     Performance means using your physical competencies with your knowledge of a physical activity to produce an effective and successful result. An example of success for an attacking player in a game of football would be scoring a goal.

     (3 marks)

3   Describe the qualities needed to be effective in the role of team captain.

     Team captains need to be highly skilled in their sport so they can be a role model for their team-mates, as well as being able to evaluate team member's performances. They should have good leadership and motivational qualities, and be able to communicate clearly. They also need to be organised, as they may need to organise matches or organise players during a match.

     (6 marks)

Exam Questions

1   Each of the following is needed for health **except**:

    A physical well-being

    B mental well-being

    C competence

    D social well-being

(1 mark)

2   In which of the following roles would someone **not** be an active participant in a physical activity?

    A spectator

    B captain

    C referee

    D player

(1 mark)

3   Ballet is a dance activity.
To be successful in ballet performance, a participant must be able to:

    A improve their social well-being.

    B outwit their opponents.

    C beat their personal best time.

    D communicate emotions though their body movement.

(1 mark)

4   Exercising regularly can help improve your health and well-being.

    a)   What is exercise?

        ....

        ....

(2 marks)

    b)   Describe **two** possible indicators or measures of a person's well-being.

        ....

        ....

        ....

(2 marks)

Exam Questions

5   A student regularly participates in physical activity by playing for a local basketball team.

a)   Describe **three** benefits that can be gained from playing basketball.

....

....

....

....

(3 marks)

b)   Regular exercise is one aspect of a healthy active lifestyle.
Describe **two** other characteristics of a healthy active lifestyle.

....

....

....

(2 marks)

c)   Basketball is a games activity. Give **one** example of a success in this type of activity.

....

....

(1 mark)

6   Janice plays tennis for her school team. Unfortunately Janice is injured and so cannot play, but she still wants to participate in the activity.

a)   Name **one** role Janice could adopt so that she can still participate in the activity.

....

(1 mark)

b)   Describe **three** qualities Janice would need to be effective in this role.

....

....

....

....

(3 marks)

Revision Summary — Section One

Right, it's the end of the first section — well, almost. You could just call it a day and go on to the next section, but I wouldn't recommend it. Now's the perfect time to test what you've learnt and reinforce it in your brain. It really won't take that long either — and it's certainly a lot quicker than not doing it, and then having to relearn it all later. Handily, there's just happens to be a load of questions below. Don't expect to be able to answer them all straight away, but keep at it until you can answer them all.

1) What's the definition of competence?
2) What's the definition of performance?
3) How does being creative give you an advantage when you play sport?
4) Explain the meaning of:
    a) physical well-being,
    b) mental well-being,
    c) social well-being.
5) What do the letters PEASED stand for? Explain what each one means.
6) Access to green space is an indicator of good health and well-being.
    Give two other examples of how to measure health and well-being.
7) What's the definition of exercise?
8) Describe two social benefits of physical activity.
9) Describe three physical benefits of physical activity.
10) Describe five mental benefits of physical activity.
11) Explain what 'aesthetic appreciation' means.
12) What is the role of:
    a) a player/performer,
    b) an organiser.
13) Describe what a choreographer does.
14) What skills do officials need to be good at their role?
15) Explain what a coach does.
16) Explain the role of a captain.
17) Give two ways that volunteers help sport to take place.
18) Give two benefits of volunteering in sport.
19) For each of the following activities, write down a skill associated with it
    and what counts as a success in that activity:
    a) games activities,
    b) athletic activities,
    c) dance activities,
    d) gymnastic activities,
    e) survival and adventure activities,
    f) fitness and health activities.

The Skeletal System

The <u>skeleton</u> gives the body its <u>shape</u> and has loads of jobs to do. It's made up of various kinds of <u>bones</u>, all meeting at <u>joints</u> that can <u>move</u> in different ways. Here's what you need to know...

The **Skeleton** has Different **Functions**

The skeleton does a <u>lot more</u> than you might think. The main functions are:

① SUPPORT/SHAPE:

1) The skeleton is a <u>rigid bone frame</u> for the rest of the body. Our <u>shape</u> is mainly due to our <u>skeleton</u>.

2) It's important to have a <u>healthy posture</u>, e.g. not slouching, to avoid problems like back pain.

3) The skeleton <u>supports</u> the <u>soft tissues</u> like skin and muscle.

4) Without the skeleton, we'd <u>collapse</u> like jelly.

② PROTECTION:

1) Bones are very <u>tough</u>.

2) They <u>protect delicate organs</u> like the <u>brain</u>, <u>heart</u> and <u>lungs</u>.

③ MOVEMENT:

1) There are loads of <u>joints</u> — places where two or more bones meet.

2) <u>Muscles</u>, attached by <u>tendons</u>, can move various bones.

④ MAKING BLOOD CELLS:

1) <u>Long bones</u> contain <u>bone marrow</u>.

2) New <u>red blood cells</u> are made in this bone marrow.

3) Red blood cells <u>carry oxygen</u> around the body (see p19) where it's used to release <u>energy</u> (see p18).

⑤ MINERAL STORAGE:

Bones <u>store</u> important <u>minerals</u> like calcium (see p46).

Connective Tissues Join Muscle and Bones

There are <u>three types</u> of <u>connective tissue</u> you need to know about.

CARTILAGE

Cartilage forms <u>cushions between bones</u> to stop them rubbing.

LIGAMENTS

Ligaments are like very strong <u>string</u> that <u>holds bones together</u>.

TENDONS

Tendons attach <u>muscles to bones</u> (or to other muscles).

There are **Two** Different **Types** of **Joint**

There are two different <u>types</u> of joint that allow you to move:

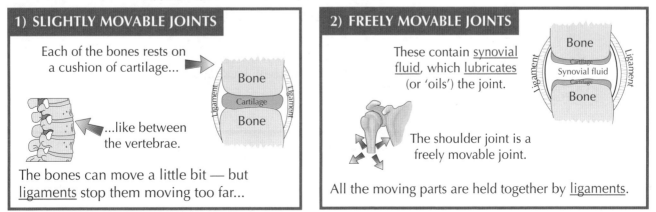

1) SLIGHTLY MOVABLE JOINTS

Each of the bones rests on a cushion of cartilage...

Bone
Cartilage
Bone

...like between the vertebrae.

The bones can move a little bit — but <u>ligaments</u> stop them moving too far...

2) FREELY MOVABLE JOINTS

These contain <u>synovial fluid</u>, which <u>lubricates</u> (or 'oils') the joint.

Bone
Cartilage
Synovial fluid
Cartilage
Bone

The shoulder joint is a freely movable joint.

All the moving parts are held together by <u>ligaments</u>.

The Skeletal System

Joints are <u>clever</u> old things — they let bits of your body move in certain directions.
You need to know the <u>kinds of movement</u> your body can make and the <u>types</u> of joint too.

There are **Five Kinds** of **Joint Movement**

There are <u>five</u> different kinds of movement the joints can allow. You need to know the info.

EXTENSION	FLEXION	ADDUCTION	ABDUCTION	ROTATION
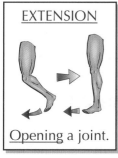	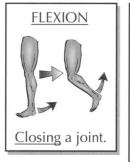		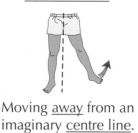	
<u>Opening</u> a joint.	<u>Closing</u> a joint.	Moving <u>towards</u> an imaginary <u>centre line</u>.	Moving <u>away</u> from an imaginary <u>centre line</u>.	<u>Turning</u> a limb <u>clockwise</u> or <u>anticlockwise</u>.

There are **Two Types** of **Freely Movable** Joint

Your shoulder and knee are both <u>freely movable joints</u> (see p11). But, your shoulder can move in more directions than your knee. That's because it's a <u>different</u> kind of freely movable joint.
There are <u>two types</u> you need to know about:

Ball and Socket

1) Your <u>hips</u> and <u>shoulders</u> are ball and socket joints.
2) These joints can move in <u>all directions</u>, and they can <u>rotate</u> as well.
3) So this allows <u>flexion</u>, <u>extension</u>, <u>adduction</u>, <u>abduction</u> and <u>rotation</u>.

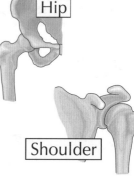

Hip

Shoulder

Actions where this type of joint is important:
<u>Shoulder</u> — bowling in cricket, arm swing in tennis.
<u>Hip</u> — any sort of running, kicking, doing the splits.

Hinge

1) Your <u>knees</u> and <u>elbows</u> are hinge joints.
2) The joint can go <u>backwards and forwards</u>, but not side-to-side.
3) This allows <u>flexion</u> and <u>extension</u>.

Elbow

Knee

Activities where you have to <u>kick</u>, <u>run</u> or <u>throw</u> all use this joint.
E.g. throwing a basket ball, kicking a football.

Joints joints joints — it's enough to make you hungry...

There's a load of names to learn here — so give it some time. It can be a bit tricky, but try to think of ways to remember things. Like this: <u>ADD</u>uction is bringing two bits together, kind of like 'adding' them — while <u>AB</u>Duction is taking them away — like when you're <u>abducted by aliens</u>.

The Muscular System

There's lots to know about the muscular system. You need to know the two different types of muscle, and the names of the bigger, or more important, muscles. Here's everything you need...

There are **Two** Different **Types** of **Muscle**

1) Like the title says, there are two different types of muscle you need to know. These are...

INVOLUNTARY MUSCLES

Around organs such as the intestines, and blood vessels. They work without conscious effort from you.

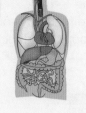

VOLUNTARY MUSCLES

They're attached to the skeleton and are under your control.

2) All muscles are made up of fibres.

3) Nerve impulses are what tell muscles to contract (or in the case of the heart, they cause it to contract in a regular pattern — the heartbeat).

4) Complex movements are made possible by the coordination of nerve impulses sent to the muscles by the nervous system.

Different Activities Work Different **Muscle Groups**

You need to know what the big important muscles are called. You also need to know which activities and movements are particularly good for each muscle. Learn this diagram well.

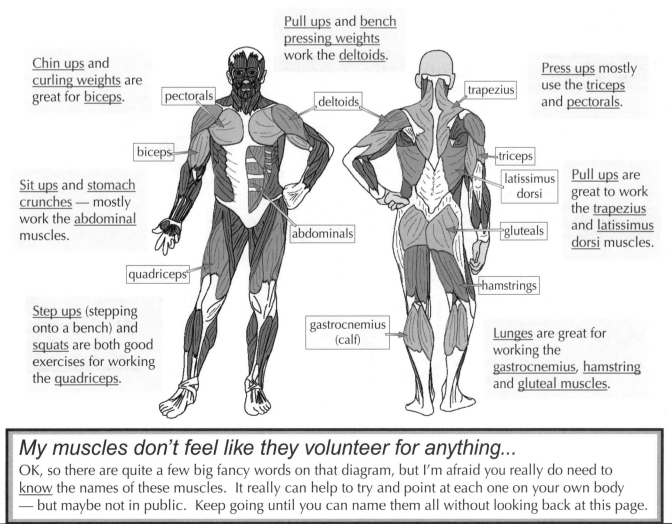

Chin ups and curling weights are great for biceps.

Pull ups and bench pressing weights work the deltoids.

Press ups mostly use the triceps and pectorals.

Sit ups and stomach crunches — mostly work the abdominal muscles.

Pull ups are great to work the trapezius and latissimus dorsi muscles.

Step ups (stepping onto a bench) and squats are both good exercises for working the quadriceps.

Lunges are great for working the gastrocnemius, hamstring and gluteal muscles.

pectorals

deltoids

trapezius

biceps

triceps

latissimus dorsi

abdominals

gluteals

quadriceps

hamstrings

gastrocnemius (calf)

My muscles don't feel like they volunteer for anything...

OK, so there are quite a few big fancy words on that diagram, but I'm afraid you really do need to know the names of these muscles. It really can help to try and point at each one on your own body — but maybe not in public. Keep going until you can name them all without looking back at this page.

The Muscular System

You need to know that muscles work in <u>pairs</u>, and all the fancy names that go with it.

Muscles *Pull* on Bones

1) Muscles used for movement are attached to <u>two different bones</u> by <u>tendons</u>.
2) Only <u>one</u> of these bones will move when the muscle contracts.

> Muscles can only do one thing — <u>pull</u>.
> To make a joint move in two directions, you need
> <u>two muscles</u> that can pull in <u>opposite directions</u>.

Antagonistic Muscles Work in *Pairs*

1) <u>Antagonistic</u> muscles are <u>pairs of muscles</u> that work <u>against</u> each other.
2) One muscle <u>contracts</u> (shortens) while the other one <u>relaxes</u> (lengthens) and <u>vice versa</u>.
3) The muscle that's doing the work (contracting) is the <u>prime mover</u>, or <u>agonist</u>.
4) The muscle that's relaxing is the <u>antagonist</u>.
5) There are also muscles called <u>synergists</u>. They hold the stationary bone still, so only one bone moves — e.g. when the bicep contracts to bend the elbow, synergists stop the shoulder moving.

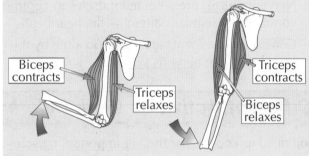

Biceps contracts — Triceps relaxes / Triceps contracts — Biceps relaxes

Your *Muscles* and *Joints* Act as *Levers*

Joints <u>multiply</u> either the <u>force</u> of a muscle, or the <u>speed</u> of a movement or both. When you bend your elbow, your muscles make a <u>short</u> movement, but your hand makes a <u>larger</u> one — this means your hand moves <u>more quickly</u>.

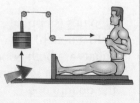

Short, slow movement / Larger, quicker movement

There are *Two Types* of *Muscle Contraction*

There are two types of <u>contraction</u> that a muscle can undergo — <u>isometric</u> and <u>isotonic</u>.

<u>ISOMETRIC CONTRACTION</u> — the muscle <u>stays the same length</u> and so nothing moves.

Like if you pull on a rope attached to a wall.

<u>ISOTONIC CONTRACTION</u> — the muscle <u>changes length</u> and so something moves.

Like if you exercise with weights that are free to move.

Antagonists — don't let them get to you...

Muscles work in pairs — while one <u>contracts</u>, the other has a nice little <u>rest</u>. All this 'antagonist' and 'agonist' stuff might sound a bit gruesome, but don't panic — it's not too bad once you've read through it a few times. Make sure you know the difference between an isotonic and an isometric contraction.

Warm-Up and Worked Exam Questions

Warm-Up Questions

1) What do bones protect — vital organs, muscles or joints?
2) Muscles can only work in one direction. Do they pull or push?
3) A hinged joint allows movement in two directions. One is flexion, what is the other?
4) Name the three types of connective tissue that join muscles and bones.
5) Give one example of a ball and socket joint.
6) What is the name given to a pair of muscles that work against each other?
7) Muscles can contract in two different ways — isometric and isotonic. Which type of contraction causes movement?

Worked Exam Question

There you have it — that pretty much wraps up bones, joints and muscles. So now would be a good time to try a few practice exam questions. Handily, there are some over the page. Here's a worked example you can read through to give you a head start...

1   This question is about the role of the skeleton.

   a)   Making blood cells is one of the functions of the skeleton.
         Name **three** other functions of the skeleton.

         Maintaining the body's shape.

         Allowing movement.

         Protecting vital organs.

         You could also put "mineral storage", but you only need three functions to get the marks.

         (3 marks)

   b)   Below are four kinds of movement that joints can allow. Complete the table below
         by naming a different joint that allows each type of movement.

Type of movement	Example of Joint
Flexion	*knee*
Extension	*elbow*
Abduction	*hip*
Adduction	*shoulder*

         There are other possible answers to this question. For example, you could swap the positions of 'hip' and 'shoulder', because both allow abduction and adduction.

         (4 marks)

Exam Questions

1   What type of joint is an elbow joint?

     A   Hinge

     B   Ball and socket

     C   Flexion

     D   Trapezius

(1 mark)

2   The diagram below shows some of the muscles in the human body.

     a)   Name the muscles labelled A-F on the diagram below.

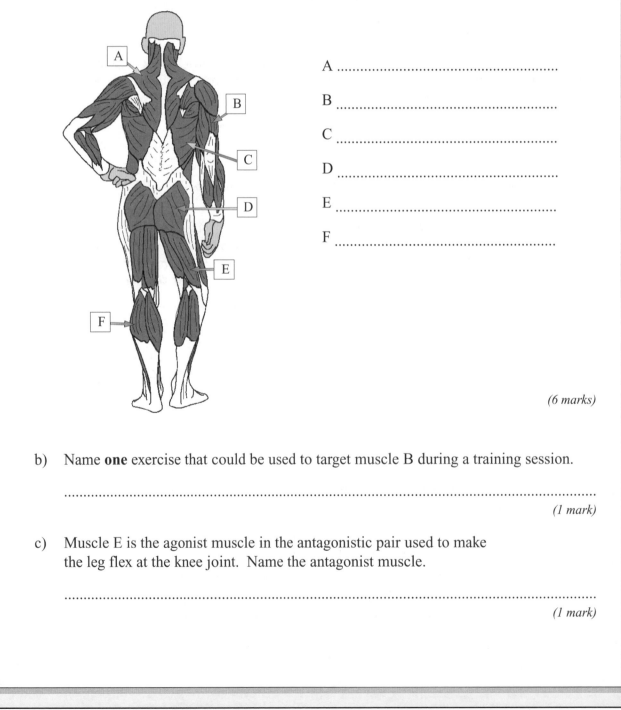

A ....

B ....

C ....

D ....

E ....

F ....

(6 marks)

     b)   Name **one** exercise that could be used to target muscle B during a training session.

....

(1 mark)

     c)   Muscle E is the agonist muscle in the antagonistic pair used to make the leg flex at the knee joint. Name the antagonist muscle.

....

(1 mark)

The Respiratory System

You'll probably recognise most of the stuff on this page from <u>biology</u> — but it's always good to have a recap. If you don't know this, then stuff like 'how <u>smoking</u> affects <u>gas exchange</u> in the <u>alveoli</u>' on page 47 is just going to sound like complete nonsense.

*The **Air** You Breathe **Ends Up** in the **Alveoli***

The respiratory system is <u>everything</u> we use to <u>breathe</u>.

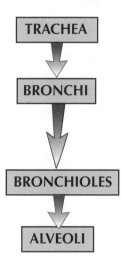

TRACHEA
BRONCHI
BRONCHIOLES
ALVEOLI

1) Air passes through the nose or mouth and then on to the <u>trachea</u>.

2) The trachea splits into two tubes called <u>bronchi</u> (each one is a '<u>bronchus</u>') — one going to each lung.

3) The bronchi split into progressively smaller tubes called <u>bronchioles</u>.

4) The bronchioles finally end at small bags called <u>alveoli</u> (each one is an '<u>alveolus</u>') where <u>gas exchange</u> takes place — see below.

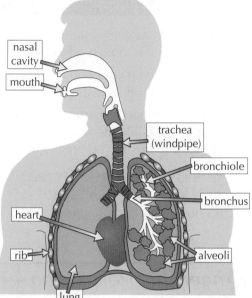

nasal cavity
mouth
trachea (windpipe)
bronchiole
bronchus
heart
alveoli
rib
lung

The area inside the chest containing the lungs, heart and all the other bits is called the <u>chest cavity</u>.

Oxygen** and **Carbon Dioxide** are **Exchanged** in the **Alveoli

There are millions of alveoli in your lungs. This is where the <u>gaseous exchange</u> happens. The alveoli are wrapped in tiny blood vessels called <u>capillaries</u>.

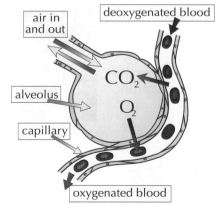

air in and out
deoxygenated blood
CO_2
O_2
alveolus
capillary
oxygenated blood

Oxygenated blood has <u>more oxygen</u> than deoxygenated blood.

When you breathe:

1) <u>Carbon dioxide</u> moves from your blood into the <u>alveoli</u>.

2) Oxygen in the alveoli moves across to the red blood cells. The red blood cells contain <u>haemoglobin</u>, which combines with the oxygen to make <u>oxyhaemoglobin</u>.

3) The red blood cells <u>carry</u> the oxygen around the body and <u>deliver</u> it to where it's needed.

4) At the same time, the blood <u>collects</u> carbon dioxide to be taken back to the lungs.

The air you breathe in and the air you breathe out are <u>different</u>. The air you breathe out has <u>less</u> oxygen, because the body's used some — but <u>more</u> carbon dioxide which is made during respiration (see p18).

Air we go — keeping trachea respiratory system...

This page is OK really — it's just got lots of tricky names that make it <u>seem</u> hard. Make sure you learn which gas goes where when you breathe, and what alveoli are. (Hint: alveoli are <u>not</u> a type of pasta.)

The Respiratory System

Once you've taken in oxygen, it's used to release energy in a process called <u>respiration</u>. Read on...

Aerobic Respiration — With Oxygen

1) <u>All</u> the living cells in your body need <u>energy</u>. Normally the body converts <u>glucose</u> (a <u>sugar</u> found in food) into <u>energy</u> using <u>oxygen</u>. This is called <u>aerobic respiration</u>.

> Glucose + Oxygen → Carbon dioxide + Water + Energy

2) If your body's keeping up with the <u>oxygen demand</u> of the cells, it means there's enough oxygen available for aerobic respiration.

3) Activities where your body can <u>keep up</u> with oxygen demand are called <u>aerobic activities</u>.

> AEROBIC ACTIVITY: 'with oxygen'. If the exercise you're doing isn't <u>too fast</u> and you're exercising at a <u>steady rate</u>, your heart and lungs can supply your muscles with all the oxygen they need.

4) You <u>breathe out</u> the carbon dioxide through your lungs, while the water is lost as <u>sweat</u>, <u>urine</u>, or in the <u>air</u> you breathe out.

5) As long as your muscles are <u>supplied with enough oxygen</u>, you can do aerobic exercise — so this is used for <u>long periods</u> of exercise.

6) It's how <u>marathon runners</u> get their energy.

Anaerobic Respiration — Without Oxygen

1) During <u>vigorous exercise</u>, your body <u>can't</u> supply all the oxygen needed. When this happens, your muscles release energy <u>without</u> using oxygen in a different process called <u>anaerobic respiration</u>.

> Glucose + No oxygen → Lactic acid + Energy

2) Activities where your body has to do this are called <u>anaerobic activities</u>.

> ANAEROBIC ACTIVITY: 'without oxygen'. If you exercise in <u>short</u>, <u>fast spurts</u>, your heart can't supply your muscles with oxygen as fast as your muscle cells use it.

3) The <u>lactic acid</u> produced in this process <u>builds up</u> after a while.

4) Lactic acid is a <u>mild poison</u> and its build-up soon makes your muscles feel <u>tired</u> — so this form of respiration only works for <u>short</u>, <u>strenuous</u> activities.

5) To get rid of the lactic acid, you need <u>oxygen</u>. The amount of <u>oxygen</u> you need is the <u>oxygen debt</u>. You breathe it in when you've stopped exercising so vigorously.

6) This is how <u>sprinters</u> get their energy.

Vital Capacity — The Most Air You Can Breathe In

1) When you breathe in and out normally, only a <u>small volume</u> of air moves in and out — the <u>tidal volume</u>.

2) You can use the tidal volume to work out the 'minute volume' — the amount of air inhaled in one minute.

minute volume = tidal volume × respiratory rate

3) Your tidal volume is only a fraction of your <u>vital capacity</u>:

VITAL CAPACITY — the most air you could possibly breathe in after breathing out the largest volume of air you can.

4) The <u>larger</u> your vital capacity, the <u>more oxygen</u> can be taken in and absorbed into your blood stream in every breath — so the oxygen supply to the muscles is increased.

The Cardiovascular System

Your cardiovascular system's made up of your <u>heart</u>, <u>lungs</u>, <u>blood</u> and <u>blood vessels</u> (<u>arteries</u>, <u>veins</u> and <u>capillaries</u>). You need to know what it does and how it does it...

The **Cardiovascular System** has **Three** Main Functions

1) `TRANSPORT` — <u>moving</u> things around the body in the bloodstream, like <u>oxygen</u>, <u>nutrients</u> (like glucose), <u>water</u> and <u>waste</u>.

2) `BODY TEMPERATURE CONTROL` — moving more blood nearer the skin <u>cools</u> the body more quickly. That's why your skin looks <u>redder</u> after exercise.

3) `PROTECTION` — moving <u>antibodies</u> around the body to fight disease. Your blood also <u>clots</u> to seal cuts.

Your **Blood** is made up of **Cells**, **Platelets** and **Plasma**

 <u>RED BLOOD CELLS</u> — Carry oxygen around the body in red <u>haemoglobin</u>. They have <u>no nucleus</u>, leaving more space for haemoglobin.

<u>WHITE BLOOD CELLS</u> — Fight <u>against</u> <u>disease</u> by destroying bacteria, viruses and toxins.

<u>PLASMA</u> — Carries everything in the bloodstream. That includes blood cells, digested food (e.g. glucose), waste (e.g. urea, carbon dioxide) and hormones.

<u>PLATELETS</u> — Small <u>fragments</u> of cells with <u>no nucleus</u>. They help blood to clot at wounds.

The **Cardiovascular System** Has a **Double Circuit**

1) The <u>cardiovascular system</u> is made up of three main parts — the <u>heart</u>, the <u>blood</u> and the <u>blood vessels</u>.

2) Each time blood goes right round your body, it goes <u>through the heart twice</u> — once through each side.

There are <u>two</u> main types of blood vessel: <u>arteries</u>,— which carry blood away from the heart, and <u>veins</u> — which carry blood towards the heart.

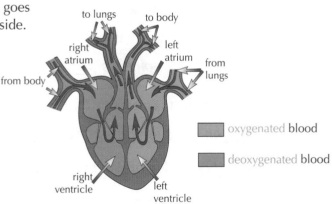

oxygenated blood

deoxygenated blood

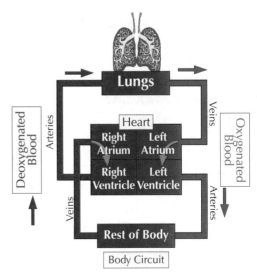

This happens because <u>there are two circuits</u>:

The <u>body circuit</u> is the main circuit. It carries:

1) oxygenated blood around the body in the <u>arteries</u>.

2) deoxygenated blood back to the heart along the <u>veins</u>.

The <u>other circuit</u> includes the heart and lungs.

1) It carries deoxygenated blood from the heart to the lungs to be oxygenated.

2) The blood then goes <u>back to the heart</u> to be pumped around the <u>body circuit</u>.

Warm-Up and Worked Exam Questions

Warm-Up Questions

1) Which gas does the body need in order to function — carbon dioxide, oxygen or methane?
2) Which type of blood cell carries oxygen around the body — red or white?
3) Which sugar is the starting material for both aerobic respiration and anaerobic respiration?
4) Which type of respiration uses oxygen — aerobic or anaerobic?
5) Name the waste product formed during anaerobic respiration.
6) What is 'tidal volume'?
7) Which type of blood vessel carries blood away from the heart?

Worked Exam Questions

Look through these worked examples, then have a go at the exam-style questions on page 21.

1   List the **three** functions of the circulatory system.

Transportation (of oxygen/nutrients/water/waste).

Control of body temperature.

Protection from disease.

(3 marks)

2   Tom sprints for 200 m.
     While Tom sprints, his muscles build up an oxygen debt.

   a)   i) What type of respiration occurs while Tom is sprinting?

   Anaerobic respiration

   ii) Explain what is meant by the term 'oxygen debt'.

   Oxygen debt is the 'extra' oxygen needed after vigorous exercise

   has stopped in order to get rid of the lactic acid produced during

   anaerobic respiration.

   Here you get one mark for saying it's the extra oxygen needed to make up   *(2 marks)*
   the shortfall after vigorous exercise, and another for mentioning lactic acid removal.

   b)   As Tom runs, his body temperature increases.
        Describe how his cardiovascular system helps to control his body temperature.

   By moving more blood closer to the surface of the skin.

   (1 mark)

Exam Questions

1   Where in the respiratory system are carbon dioxide and oxygen exchanged?

    A Bronchi

    B Trachea

    C Bronchioles

    D Alveoli

(1 mark)

2   a)   What is meant by the term 'vital capacity'?

....

(1 mark)

    b)   Explain how having a large vital capacity could be an advantage when participating in a physical activity.

....

....

....

(3 marks)

3   Long-distance running is an aerobic activity.

    a)   Explain what is meant by an 'aerobic activity'.

....

....

(2 marks)

    b)   Write a chemical word equation to show the process of aerobic respiration.

....

(2 marks)

4   a)   Describe the conditions under which anaerobic respiration occurs.

....

....

(1 mark)

    b) Name the by-product of anaerobic respiration. Describe how it affects performance.

....

....

(2 marks)

Exercise and The Cardiovascular System

When you start to <u>exercise</u>, your body has to make sure that your muscles get the <u>oxygen</u> they need so they can keep working. It also has to avoid <u>overheating</u>. It's all clever stuff.

Cardiac Output — Volume of Blood per Minute

1) Your <u>heart rate</u> is the number of times your heart beats <u>each minute</u>.

2) Your <u>stroke volume</u> is the amount of blood each ventricle pumps with <u>each contraction</u> (or heartbeat).

3) You can <u>multiply</u> your heart rate and stroke volume to work out the volume of blood pumped by a <u>ventricle per minute</u>. This is your <u>cardiac output</u>. There's more on heart rate on page 68.

HEART RATE	×	STROKE VOLUME	=	CARDIAC OUTPUT
HR	×	SV	=	CO

The Blood is Under Pressure

1) Every time your heart contracts, it <u>forces</u> blood around your body by <u>increasing</u> your <u>blood pressure</u>.

> **BLOOD PRESSURE** is the force caused by the blood on the walls of the blood vessels.

2) Your blood pressure <u>decreases</u> as it travels around each circuit — so the pressure in your <u>arteries</u> is <u>larger</u> than that in your <u>veins</u>.

Arteries have thicker and stronger walls than veins to cope with the higher pressure.

artery   vein

3) Blood pressure can be measured using a <u>sphygmomanometer</u>. It gives two readings:

<u>SYSTOLIC PRESSURE</u> — the pressure of the blood in the arteries when the left ventricle <u>contracts</u>.
<u>DIASTOLIC PRESSURE</u> — the pressure of the blood in the arteries when the left ventricle <u>relaxes</u>.

Your Body Moves Up a Gear When You Exercise

When you exercise, blood is <u>redistributed</u> around the body to <u>increase</u> the supply of <u>oxygen</u> to your <u>muscles</u> — this known as '<u>blood shunting</u>' or '<u>vascular shunting</u>'.

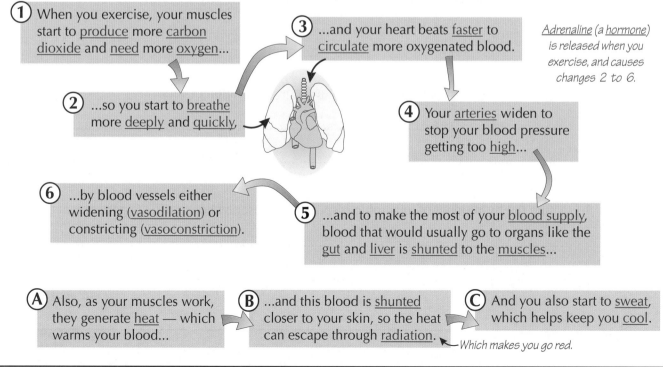

① When you exercise, your muscles start to <u>produce</u> more <u>carbon dioxide</u> and <u>need</u> more <u>oxygen</u>...

③ ...and your heart beats <u>faster</u> to <u>circulate</u> more oxygenated blood.

Adrenaline (a hormone) is released when you exercise, and causes changes 2 to 6.

② ...so you start to <u>breathe</u> more <u>deeply</u> and <u>quickly</u>,

④ Your <u>arteries</u> widen to stop your blood pressure getting too <u>high</u>...

⑥ ...by blood vessels either widening (<u>vasodilation</u>) or constricting (<u>vasoconstriction</u>).

⑤ ...and to make the most of your <u>blood supply</u>, blood that would usually go to organs like the <u>gut</u> and <u>liver</u> is <u>shunted</u> to the <u>muscles</u>...

Ⓐ Also, as your muscles work, they generate <u>heat</u> — which warms your blood...

Ⓑ ...and this blood is <u>shunted</u> closer to your skin, so the heat can escape through <u>radiation</u>. *Which makes you go red.*

Ⓒ And you also start to <u>sweat</u>, which helps keep you <u>cool</u>.

Short-Term Effects of Exercise

During exercise, your <u>muscles</u>, <u>lungs</u> and <u>heart</u> all work harder. If you're doing the AQA courses you can skip the next couple of pages on the effects of exercise.

You Need to know the **Short-Term** Effects of Exercise

The **Muscular** System

1) Whatever type of exercise you do, your <u>muscles will contract</u> — either <u>isometrically</u> or <u>isotonically</u> (see p14).

2) As you exercise, the <u>temperature</u> of your muscles <u>rises</u>.

3) Your muscles work harder than usual during exercise, so they need <u>more energy</u>.

4) Your respiratory and cardiovascular systems quickly adapt to try to provide this — see below.

5) If your body can't keep up with the oxygen demand, your muscles will respire anaerobically (see p18) and produce <u>lactic acid</u>. If you use your muscles like this for long they feel <u>tired</u>. This is <u>muscle fatigue</u>.

The **Respiratory** System

1) Your <u>breathing rate increases</u> to increase your oxygen intake.

2) You also breathe <u>more deeply</u> than normal (tidal volume increases). This means you take in more oxygen with each breath.

3) If you've been doing <u>anaerobic activity</u>, your breathing rate and depth will remain high until you've taken in enough <u>oxygen</u> to 'pay off' your <u>oxygen debt</u>.

The **Cardiovascular** System

1) Just like your breathing, your <u>heart rate increases</u> to <u>increase</u> the blood supply to your muscles.

2) Your heart also <u>contracts more strongly</u> (stroke volume increases) to pump even more blood around the body. This <u>increases</u> your <u>blood pressure</u>:

> The <u>more strongly</u> your heart <u>contracts</u>, the higher your <u>systolic</u> blood pressure will be. But your <u>diastolic</u> blood pressure usually stays the <u>same</u>.

3) Your heart rate will remain higher than normal until any <u>oxygen debt</u> is paid off.

Your Muscles Need to **Rest and Recover** after Exercise

1) After an exercise session, your muscles need time to <u>adapt</u> and <u>recover</u>.

2) If you don't rest for long enough, you could risk <u>injuring</u> yourself (see next page).

3) There are good and bad ways of <u>speeding up</u> the time it takes your muscles to <u>recover</u>...

— DIET —
Your muscles are made up of <u>proteins</u>. By eating a high protein diet, you can <u>speed up</u> the rate at which your body can <u>build</u> and <u>repair muscle</u> — <u>shortening</u> your <u>rest</u> and <u>recovery time</u>.

— DRUGS —
<u>Steroids</u> stimulate the body to produce muscle proteins at a faster rate. This also speeds up the time it takes to build and repair muscles.

Some athletes <u>illegally</u> use steroids so they can train harder and <u>improve their performance</u> (see p48).

Give your brain a quick exercise — learn this page...

We all feel a bit tired after a run, but you need to know more about the effects of exercise on the body. Make sure you know all the <u>short-term effects</u> of exercise on each of your three main body systems.

Long-Term Effects of Exercise

Regular exercise makes your body more <u>efficient</u> and <u>stronger</u>, and helps prevent nasty <u>bone</u> and <u>joint problems</u>. Remember, if you're doing an AQA course you don't need to know the stuff on this page.

Exercising Regularly has Many *Long-Term* Benefits

The **Muscular** System

1) Exercise and strength training make your muscles <u>adapt</u> — your <u>muscle fibres</u> get <u>stronger</u> and your muscle gets <u>thicker</u>. This thickening of muscles is called <u>hypertrophy</u>.

2) Your <u>strength</u> will <u>increase</u> — the thicker the muscle and the stronger the muscle fibres, the <u>more strongly</u> the muscle can contract.

3) Your tolerance to <u>lactic acid</u> build-up in your muscles also <u>increases</u>.

The **Respiratory** System

1) The muscles around your chest get <u>stronger</u> — so they can make your <u>chest cavity</u> larger.

2) With a larger chest cavity, you can breathe <u>more air</u> in — so your <u>vital capacity</u> increases.

3) The bigger your vital capacity, the more oxygen you can take in with <u>one breath</u>. This means the <u>oxygen supply</u> to your muscles will be <u>better</u> — so you'll be able to keep up vigorous exercise for <u>longer</u>.

The **Cardiovascular** System

1) Your heart is just a muscle — when you exercise it <u>adapts</u>, getting <u>bigger</u> and <u>stronger</u>.

2) A bigger, stronger heart will contract more <u>strongly</u> and pump <u>more</u> blood with each beat — so your <u>stroke volume increase</u>. This means your <u>cardiac output</u> increases too (see p15).

3) The larger your <u>stroke volume</u>, the less often your heart has to beat to pump the same amount of blood around your body. That means your <u>resting heart rate decreases</u>.

4) Physical activity also keeps your <u>blood vessels healthy</u> — your veins and arteries get <u>bigger</u> and <u>stretchier</u>, so your <u>blood pressure falls</u>.

5) The blood vessels also get <u>stronger</u>, so they're less likely to <u>burst</u> under pressure.

Regular Exercise Keeps Your *Bones* and *Joints Healthy*

<u>Exercising</u> regularly has great <u>long-term benefits</u> for both your joints and bones:

1) Exercise makes your <u>ligaments</u> and <u>tendons stronger</u>. Just like muscles, your ligaments and tendons <u>adapt</u> when you exercise. Having stronger ligaments and tendons means you're less likely to <u>injure</u> yourself, or develop <u>joint problems</u> like <u>inflammation</u> and <u>osteoarthritis</u>.

2) It increases your <u>bone density</u>. The <u>denser</u> your bones, the <u>stronger</u> they are. The stronger your bones, the <u>less likely</u> they are to <u>break</u> or <u>fracture</u>.

> <u>Osteoporosis</u> is a disease where your <u>bone density</u> is so <u>low</u>, your bones are <u>fragile</u> and <u>easily fracture</u>. It often happens in old age when the body is less able to strengthen bone. You can help prevent osteoporosis by doing <u>weight-bearing</u> exercises (where your <u>legs support</u> your weight) such as <u>walking</u>, <u>running</u>, <u>tennis</u> and <u>aerobics</u>.

Some shocking news — exercise is good for you...

It seems a bit funny at first — to stop your bones becoming weak and easily breakable, make sure that you put a large force through them. But it does make sense when you stop and think about it. Remember — the best exercises to strengthen your bones are <u>weight-bearing exercises</u>.

Warm-Up and Worked Exam Questions

Warm-Up Questions

1) What is stroke volume?
2) How could you calculate your cardiac output?
3) What effect does exercise have on your breathing rate?
4) What happens to your heart rate when you exercise?
5) What is the definition of blood pressure?
6) What is the difference between systolic and diastolic blood pressure?
7) Why does the body redirect blood flow during physical activity? What is this process called?

Worked Exam Questions

Here's another load of questions to have a go at. The first ones are done for you.

1   Exercise causes changes to the body.
     List **three** short-term effects of exercise on the human body.

Heart rate increases.

Breathing gets deeper .

Blood pressure increases.

(3 marks)

2   Give **one** long-term effect of regular exercise on the muscular system.
     Explain how this could be an advantage when participating in a physical activity.

Muscle tolerance of lactic acid increases. This will mean that you

will be able to participate in vigorous exercise for longer without

your muscles getting tired. *You could also have said that your muscle fibres*
get thicker, which make you stronger.

(2 marks)

3   Describe the long-term effects of regular exercise on the cardiovascular system.

The heart muscle gets bigger and stronger. This increases the

stroke volume and cardiac output. Resting pulse rate will decrease.

Blood vessels get stronger, bigger and stretchier. This will also

cause blood pressure to fall.

This question's worth 5 marks — so make sure you give at least 5 points.

(5 marks)

Exam Questions

1   Which of the following is an immediate effect of exercise on the cardiovascular system?

    A   Increased vital capacity

    B   Increased stroke volume

    C   Increased tidal volume

    D   Decreased heart rate

(1 mark)

2   Why is it important to allow time to rest between exercise sessions?

....

....

....

(3 marks)

3   Osteoporosis is a bone condition that affects many people as they get older.

    a)   Explain how regular participation in weight-bearing activities can help prevent osteoporosis.

....

....

(2 marks)

    b)   Give **two** examples of weight-bearing exercises.

....

....

(2 marks)

4   Exercise affects the body in many ways, both immediately and in the long term.

    a)   Describe the long-term effects of regular exercise on the respiratory system.

....

....

....

(3 marks)

    b)   Why do breathing rate and heart rate often remain high for a while after exercise has stopped?

....

....

(2 marks)

Revision Summary — Section Two

Well done — you've made it through to the end of another section. To make sure you know all you need to about the joys of the human body and the effects of exercise, have a go at these questions. Keep going through them until you know your hinge joints from your ball and socket joints, and can answer all the questions without having to sneak a look back at the section.

1) Name five functions of the skeleton.

2) What type of connective tissue joins bones to bones? What's the point of cartilage?

3) Are muscles attached to bones by: a) ligaments, b) tendons, c) cartilage, or d) sheep?

4) Draw a picture of: a) a slightly movable joint, and b) a freely movable joint.

5) Name the five different types of joint movement, and describe each of them.

6) Name two types of movable joint.

7) Say what kinds of movement each type of movable joint will allow.
   Give an example of an action or activity that relies on that type of joint.

8) Name the two different types of muscle, and give an example of each type.
   What is the difference between them?

9) What are the main muscles of the human body? Either label a sketch, or make sure you can name them on your own body. You should be able to name 11 muscle groups.

10) An antagonist relaxes while an agonist does work. TRUE or FALSE?

11) What's a synergist, and what does it do?

12) Do muscles and joints act as: a) levers, b) pulleys, or c) cranes?

13) What are isotonic and isometric contractions?

14) Draw a rough sketch of the chest cavity, and mark on all the bits of the respiratory system.

15) Where does gaseous exchange take place? What gases are exchanged?

16) Describe aerobic and anaerobic respiration. Give examples of aerobic and anaerobic activities.

17) Why do you still need lots of oxygen after you've finished exercising hard?

18) Explain the term 'vital capacity'.

19) Name the three main functions of the cardiovascular system.

20) What part of your blood carries oxygen around the body?

21) Explain why every blood cell goes through the heart twice on its way round the body.

22) Describe what is meant by a) heart rate, and b) stroke volume.

23) Write down an equation to calculate your cardiac output from your heart rate and stroke volume.

24) What is 'blood pressure'? What are the two readings given when blood pressure is measured? Why are they different?

25) What changes take place in the body to increase the supply of oxygen to your muscles when you start to exercise?

26) What substance is responsible for these changes, and what type of substance is it?

27) What does 'blood shunting' mean? How does it help you to stay cool when exercising?

28) List the short-term effects of exercise on a) the muscular system, b) the respiratory system, and c) the cardiovascular system. Now write down the long-term effects on these systems too.

29) Give two ways that the body's recovery from exercise can be speeded up.

30) Describe how exercise can prevent joint and bone problems such as osteoporosis.

Health and Fitness

There are <u>two</u> different kinds of fitness — you need one sort to be able to do everyday activities like walking up stairs, and the other to be good at a sports activity. You need to know about both...

Fitness can be **Health-Related** or **Skill-Related**

Fitness means being physically able to meet the <u>demands of your environment</u>.

1) So fitness just means that you're able to do whatever you <u>want</u> or <u>need</u> to do, without getting tired too quickly.

2) There are two basic kinds of fitness — <u>health-related fitness</u> and <u>skill-related fitness</u>.

HEALTH-RELATED FITNESS:	SKILL-RELATED FITNESS:
This means you're <u>healthy</u>, and can do <u>everyday activities</u> without feeling <u>too tired</u>. It includes: 1) <u>Cardiovascular endurance/fitness</u> — your muscles can get enough oxygen to work properly. 2) <u>Muscular strength</u> — you're strong enough to lift, push, pull, etc. 3) <u>Muscular endurance</u> — your muscles don't get tired too quickly. 4) <u>Flexibility</u> — how far you can move different parts of your body. 5) <u>Body composition</u> — you shouldn't be too fat or too thin. 	This is fitness to play a sport at a <u>high level</u>. You need a <u>high level</u> of <u>health-related fitness</u>, as well as some or all of these: 1) <u>Agility</u> — to change direction quickly. 2) <u>Balance</u> — to remain stable. 3) <u>Coordination</u> — to move accurately and smoothly. 4) Fast <u>reactions</u> — to respond quickly. 5) <u>Speed</u>. 6) <u>Power</u> — brute strength combined with speed.

Make sure you know whether each component is health-related or skill-related. More on these components coming up...

You can be **Fit Without** Being **Healthy**

1) Health-related <u>fitness</u> is an important part of a <u>healthy, active lifestyle</u>.

2) But you can have a high level of <u>fitness</u> without being <u>physically healthy</u>.

> E.g. if your body doesn't get the <u>right nutrients</u> through eating a <u>balanced diet</u>, you won't be <u>healthy</u> — even if you're <u>fit</u> through doing <u>exercise</u>.
> <u>Drug</u> use is <u>banned</u> in most sports, but some incredibly fit athletes still use them to improve their performance (see p48). This can have a huge impact on their health.

3) Don't forget — <u>physical</u> health and fitness are only <u>one</u> bit of <u>health</u>. Health also includes your <u>social</u> and <u>mental well-being</u> (see p1). It doesn't matter how physically fit you are — if you're permanently <u>unhappy</u>, you're <u>not</u> healthy.

Feeling fit and healthy ready for this section...

So, you can be fit and healthy, but just because you're fit, it doesn't mean you're healthy (although quite often being fit helps). Make sure you know the <u>definition</u> of 'fitness' — the examiners like to ask multiple choice questions on what key words like <u>fitness</u>, <u>health</u> and <u>exercise</u> mean.

Endurance and Stamina

Endurance is how long you can do something before you get tired. You need to know about two different types — cardiovascular endurance and muscular endurance. They're both to do with your muscles.

Cardiovascular Endurance Involves your Heart and Lungs

1) Cardiovascular (CV) endurance, cardiovascular fitness and cardiovascular stamina are all different names for the same thing — they're all about keeping your muscles supplied with oxygen.

> **CARDIOVASCULAR ENDURANCE/FITNESS/STAMINA**
> is the ability to exercise your whole body for a long time.

2) If your heart and lungs can provide a lot of oxygen, your cardiovascular endurance is good. It means you can exercise your whole body for a long time without getting too tired.

3) As your muscles work harder, they need more oxygen — so your breathing and heart rate get faster to move more oxygen around the body.

4) The more efficient your cardiovascular system is, the slower your pulse rate will be (both while resting and exercising), and the quicker it will return to normal after exercise.

5) To improve your cardiovascular endurance, you have to work your heart and lungs hard for at least 15 minutes. This usually means exercising with your heart rate between 60% and 80% of its maximum (see p69).

Muscular Strength — the Force a Muscle can Exert

1) Muscular strength is just how strong your muscles are (unsurprisingly).

> **MUSCULAR STRENGTH** is the amount of force that a muscle can apply.

2) Strength is very important in sports where you need to push or pull things using a lot of force, like weightlifting and judo.

3) There are lots of things in everyday life that need strength — like carrying bags of shopping or lifting a small child. Strength is a component of health-related fitness (see p28).

4) If your muscles are strong you're also less likely to injure yourself by picking something up that's heavy.

Muscular Endurance — How Long 'til You get Tired

1) When your voluntary muscles (see p13) have been overworked, they get tired and start to feel heavy or weak.

> **MUSCULAR ENDURANCE** is the ability to repeatedly use your voluntary muscles over a long time, without getting tired.

2) Muscular endurance is really important in any physical activity where you're using the same muscles repeatedly — e.g. in racquet sports like squash where you have to repeatedly swing your arm.

Your muscles are made up of two different types of fibre. One type (fast twitch fibres) contract very quickly and very powerfully — but they get tired quickly. The second type of fibre (slow twitch fibres) contract more slowly and with less force — but they don't get tired as quickly and so are better for muscular endurance.

The things I have to endure...
CV and muscular endurance are both about your muscles, but CV endurance is about getting oxygen to them, while muscular endurance is how long they can go for. Learn the difference between them.

Flexibility and Body Composition

Flexibility and suppleness are the same thing, and depend on your joints and muscles. They're both about how bendy you are — whether you struggle to touch your toes or you can twist like a pretzel.

Flexibility is your Range of Movement

1) Flexibility is to do with how far your joints move. This depends on the type of joint and the 'stretchiness' of the muscles around it.

> **FLEXIBILITY** is the amount of movement possible at a joint.

2) It's often forgotten about, but flexibility is dead useful for any physical activity. Here's why...

FEWER INJURIES:
If you're flexible, you're less likely to pull or strain a muscle or stretch too far and injure yourself.

BETTER POSTURE:
More flexibility means a better posture and fewer aches and pains.
Bad posture can lead to permanent deformity of the spine, as well as straining your back.
It can also impair breathing.

BETTER PERFORMANCE:
You can't do some sports without being flexible — e.g. gymnastics and dance. Flexibility makes you more efficient in other sports like swimming or hurdling — so you use less energy.

Your Body Composition — % of Fat, Muscle and Bone

> **BODY COMPOSITION** — the percentages of your body weight made up by fat, muscle and bone.

1) If you're healthy, your body will normally be made up of between 15% and 25% body fat.

2) Having too much body fat makes physical activities harder to do.

3) The increased strain on your muscles and joints means you have a higher risk of injuring yourself.

Having a high percentage of body fat often means you have a poor diet, which could lead to other health problems, e.g. heart trouble.

Your BMI is Based on your Height and Weight

1) Your Body Mass Index (BMI) is calculated using your height and weight — you divide your weight (in kg) by your height squared (in metres).

2) It gives you an idea of whether you are underweight, a healthy weight, overweight or obese.

3) However, your BMI doesn't take into account your body composition — athletes like weightlifters will have a high BMI due to the size of their muscles, but it doesn't mean they're actually obese.

BMI	
< 18.5	Underweight
18.5 - 25	Healthy weight
25 - 30	Overweight
> 30	Obese

Body composition — muscle, bone and flab...

You can increase your flexibility (and reduce your risk of getting injured) by warming up (see page 60) and stretching before you get stuck into doing a physical activity. Make sure you learn the definition of body composition, as well as what BMI is and why it might be misleading.

Strength, Speed and Power

Strength, speed and power are all different, but they're closely linked.

There are Three Kinds of Strength

There's more to being strong than just being able to lift heavy objects — there are three different kinds of strength. You'll have a mixture of all three.

STATIC STRENGTH	EXPLOSIVE STRENGTH	DYNAMIC STRENGTH
• You use static strength to exert force on a stationary object. • Your muscles stay the same length, so there's not much movement. • It's useful in arm-wrestling and a rugby scrum.	• You use explosive strength to exert force in one very brief, but very fast movement. • It's closely linked to power (see p32). • It's useful for the javelin or high jump.	• You use dynamic strength to apply force repeatedly over a long time. • It's linked to endurance. • It's useful for doing loads of press-ups or cycling.

Most sports need all three kinds of strength — but they're usually not all equally important.

Speed is How Quickly You Move

1) Speed is a measure of how quickly you cover a distance.

2) It can also be how quickly you can carry out a movement, e.g. how quickly you can throw a punch, run a mile or carry out any physical tasks.

3) To work out speed, you just divide the distance covered by the time taken to do it. A fancy way of saying this is 'differential rate'.

4) Speed is important in lots of activities — from the obvious, like a 100 m sprint, to the less obvious, like the speed a hockey player can swing their arm to whack a ball across the pitch.

5) Speed is a component of skill-related fitness, but it can improve your lifestyle too. E.g. being able to do physical jobs quickly means you'll have more leisure time (see p92) to socialise or play sport.

> **SPEED** is the rate at which someone is able to move, or cover a distance in a given amount of time.

— **REACTION TIME** —
This is the time it takes you to respond to something (see next page).

For speed, you need:
1) Fast reaction times,
2) Fast movement times.

— **MOVEMENT TIME** —
This is the time it takes you to carry out a certain movement — e.g. a 100 m sprint, or a shot at goal.

You can Increase Your Speed and Reactions By Training

1) You can train to improve your overall speed by improving your cardiovascular endurance. That way you can keep going at speed for longer before getting tired and having to slow down.

2) You can also improve speed by improving the power your muscles can produce (see next page).

3) You can also get quicker by improving your reactions using drills (see p76). E.g. table tennis players can practice rallies whilst standing close to the table so they have less time to react and hit the ball.

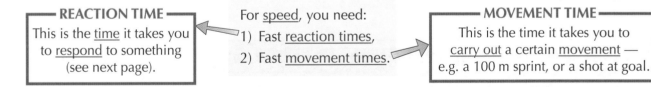

Movement time now — onto the next page...
Another page with lots on it. The names of the different kinds of strength give you clues about the differences between them. Remember, speed includes both movement time and reaction time.

Strength, Speed and Power

Quick <u>reactions</u> and <u>timing</u> can be just as important as speed, strength, and power in a physical activity.

*Reaction Time is the **Time** it Takes You to **Start Moving***

REACTION TIME is the <u>time</u> it takes you to <u>move in response</u> to something (a '<u>stimulus</u>').

1) In many sports and activities, you need to have <u>fast reactions</u> to do well.

2) The <u>stimulus</u> you respond to could be a <u>starter gun</u>, a <u>pass</u> in football...

3) You need fast reactions to be able to <u>hit a ball</u> or <u>dodge a punch</u>.
   It doesn't matter how fast you can move, if you don't react in time you'll miss or get hit.

4) Having fast reactions can effectively give you a <u>head start</u>.

Getting away quickly at the start of a <u>sprint</u> can be the difference between winning and losing.

Having faster reactions in team sports can help you <u>get away</u> from your opponents, so you can get into better playing positions.

Timing is Important too

1) It's not just your <u>reaction time</u> that matters in sports — your <u>timing</u> is important too.

2) This means things like <u>judging</u> when to <u>pass a ball</u> in football, or when to <u>take off</u> in high jump, or when to <u>overtake</u> in a race.

3) In <u>team games</u>, it's based on your judgements of <u>other people's</u> reaction times — whether it's your team-mates or players from the other team. E.g. if you think you know when someone's going to pass a ball in netball, you can make sure you're there to catch or intercept it.

4) Timing is an example of <u>strategy</u> (a plan of how you're going to win or do well) and <u>decision making</u> — you need to be good at both to do well in sports. E.g. when to push for the finish in a race — too early and you might get overtaken before the end, too late and you might not be able to catch the people in front.

*Power Means **Speed** and **Strength** Together*

<u>Power</u> is a combination of <u>speed</u> and <u>strength</u>. You can develop power by doing <u>plyometrics</u> (see p65).

POWER is ability to do <u>strength</u> movements <u>quickly</u>.   <u>power</u> = <u>strength</u> × <u>speed</u>

Most sports need power for some things — even ones like <u>golf</u>, where it's not obvious.

SPORT	YOU NEED POWER TO...
Football	...shoot
Golf	...drive
Table tennis	...smash
Tennis	...serve and smash
Cricket	...bowl fast and bat

<u>Coordination</u> and <u>balance</u> also help make the most of power — it's <u>not</u> just strength and speed you need.

You have the power...
Don't get reaction time and timing mixed up. For example in football, you have to time your run correctly, but it's having a quick reaction time that means you'll be able to get away from the player marking you.

Skill-Related Fitness

There are <u>three</u> more components of <u>skill-related fitness</u> to learn — <u>agility</u>, <u>balance</u> and <u>coordination</u>. Unless you're doing an OCR course — which means you can move straight on to the next page.

*Agility is **Control** Over Your Body's Movement*

AGILITY is the ability to control the <u>movement</u> of your <u>entire body</u>, and to be able to <u>change</u> your body's <u>position quickly</u>.

Agility is important in any activity where you've got to run about, <u>changing direction</u> all the time, like <u>football</u> or <u>hockey</u>.

*Balance is More Than **Not Wobbling***

Having a good sense of <u>balance</u> means you <u>don't wobble</u> or <u>fall over</u> easily. Great. Unfortunately you have to know a slightly fancier definition of balance for your exam.

BALANCE is the ability to keep your <u>centre of mass</u> over a <u>base support</u>.

1) You can think of the <u>mass</u> of any object as being <u>concentrated</u> at just <u>one point</u>. This point is called the <u>centre of mass</u> (or <u>centre of gravity</u>).

2) If you <u>support</u> an object at its centre of mass (e.g. <u>by hanging</u> it by that point), the object will be perfectly <u>balanced</u>.

3) <u>Everything</u> has a centre of mass — and that includes <u>us</u>.

4) As you change body position, the <u>location</u> of your centre of mass will change too.

5) Whatever activity you're doing, you need to have your centre of mass <u>over</u> whatever is <u>supporting</u> you (your <u>base support</u>) to <u>balance</u>. If you don't, you'll <u>fall over</u>.

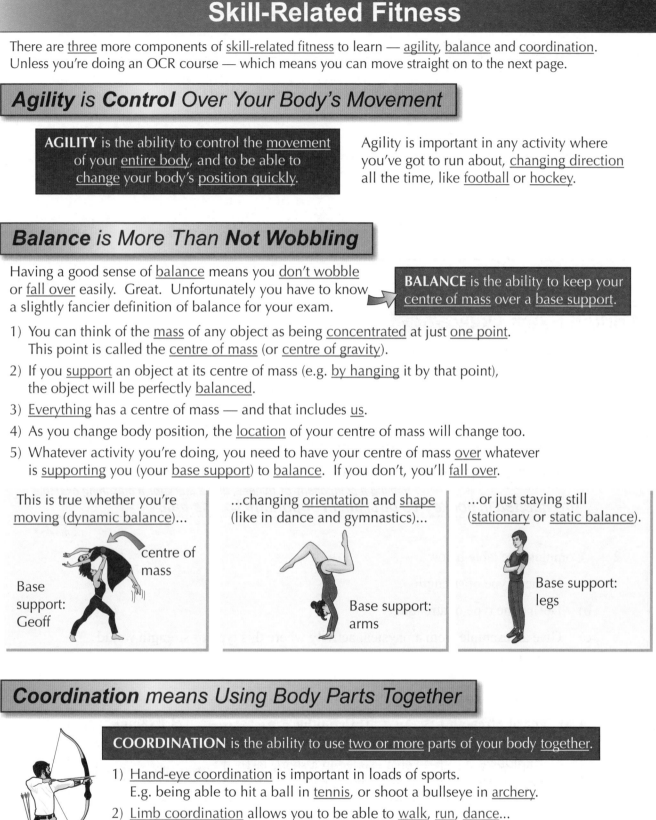

This is true whether you're <u>moving</u> (<u>dynamic balance</u>)...

centre of mass

Base support: Geoff

...changing <u>orientation</u> and <u>shape</u> (like in dance and gymnastics)...

Base support: arms

...or just staying still (<u>stationary</u> or <u>static balance</u>).

Base support: legs

Coordination means Using Body Parts Together

COORDINATION is the ability to use <u>two or more</u> parts of your body <u>together</u>.

1) <u>Hand-eye coordination</u> is important in loads of sports. E.g. being able to hit a ball in <u>tennis</u>, or shoot a bullseye in <u>archery</u>.

2) <u>Limb coordination</u> allows you to be able to <u>walk</u>, <u>run</u>, <u>dance</u>...

3) Coordinated movements are smooth and <u>efficient</u>. E.g. a <u>runner</u> with well-coordinated arms and legs will be able to run <u>faster</u> than someone who is less coordinated.

4) Limb coordination is really important in activities like <u>gymnastics</u>, where your performance is judged on your coordination.

Learn your ABC — Agility, Balance and Coordination...

<u>Agility</u>, <u>balance</u> and <u>coordination</u> all go together really. Without being able to coordinate your limbs, you're almost bound to be unbalanced and fall flat on your face. Make sure you know the definitions of each component, as well some examples of activities each one is important in.

Warm-Up and Worked Exam Questions

Warm-Up Questions

1) What is the difference between health-related and skill-related fitness?
2) Define body composition.
3) What does a person's BMI indicate?
4) Which one of the following needs explosive strength — being a member of the pack in a rugby scrum, a sprinter leaving the starting blocks or doing a set of press-ups?
5) What is meant by 'reaction time'?
6) What is power a combination of?
7) Explain why good timing is important in a cycle race.

Worked Exam Questions

Go through these questions, and then have a go at the ones on the next page on your own.
The more practice you do, the easier it gets...

1   Name **one** component of skill-related fitness. Give **one** example of how this component would give a player an advantage in a physical activity.

Component: speed. *Of course, there are many other possible answers. You'll get a mark for naming a component of fitness, and a mark for a matching example.*
It's needed in hockey to outrun an opponent to the ball.

(2 marks)

2   Complete the table below.

a)   Name a type of strength.

b)   Define the type of strength.

c)   Give an example from a physical activity where this type of strength would be an advantage.

a) Type of Strength	b) Definition	c) Example
Explosive Strength	Force exerted in a short, fast movement	Throwing a javelin
Dynamic Strength	Force applied repeatedly over a long time	Press-ups
Static Strength	Force exerted on an immovable object	Arm-wrestle

(6 marks)

Exam Questions

1   Fitness is:

    A   training regularly.

    B   the physical ability to meet the demands of the environment.

    C   a state of complete mental, physical and social well-being, and not merely the absence of disease and infirmity.

    D   the ability to exercise your whole body for a long time.

(1 mark)

2   Which of the following components of fitness is **least** important when throwing a shotput?

    A   Power

    B   Muscular strength

    C   Coordination

    D   Cardiovascular endurance

(1 mark)

3   What is meant by the term 'muscular endurance'?
Give **one** example of the importance of muscular endurance in a physical activity.

....

....

(2 marks)

4   Explain how it is possible to be fit without being healthy.

....

....

(2 marks)

5   Muscular strength is a component of health-related fitness.

    a)   Explain what is meant by 'muscular strength'.

....

(1 mark)

    b)   Explain how muscular strength can influence a healthy, active lifestyle.

....

....

(2 marks)

Exam Questions

6 Complete the table below.

a) Identify **one** component of fitness required in each sport listed.

b) Give an example of what this component is important for in the named activity.

Sport	a) Fitness Component	b) Example of use
Rugby	Strength	
Tennis		To serve and smash
Sprinting		To win the race
Gymnastics	Flexibility	

(4 marks)

7 a) Explain what is meant by the term 'agility'.

....

....

(2 marks)

b) In nearly all sports, agility, balance and coordination are required to perform well. Using a physical activity of your choice, explain the importance of these three components.

....

....

....

(3 marks)

8 Name **two** aspects of fitness that would be important for a squash player. Give **one** reason for each of your choices.

....

....

....

....

(4 marks)

Age and Performance

Age can affect performance in most sports. To make it fair, different ages often compete separately (e.g. kids won't compete against adults). You don't need to learn this page if you're on an Edexcel or WJEC course.

Age can Affect **Performance** in Sport...

STRENGTH

You don't reach your maximum strength until you're fully grown — usually at about 20. In your 20s and 30s, it's still easy to build more muscle. After this, protein levels and muscle mass fall, strength declines and it's harder to build muscle.

INJURY & DISEASE

Older people are more likely to injure themselves and it takes longer for them to recover from an injury. Older people generally suffer more from diseases too — cancer and heart disease, for example.

OXYGEN CAPACITY

This falls as you get older — so less oxygen can be taken to the muscles.

REACTION TIMES

Your reactions get slower as you get older.

EXPERIENCE

Experience is often a vital factor in sport. As you get older, you gain more experience.

FLEXIBILITY

People are most flexible in their teens, so activities like dance and gymnastics are easiest then. After the age of about 30, people generally start to become less flexible.

BUT — age doesn't matter for some sports...

If a sport depends on strength or endurance (e.g. weightlifting or marathon running), older people will often be at a disadvantage — but for less strenuous sports (e.g. golf), this doesn't have to be true.

Older competitors — low on speed, but high on experience...

Make sure you learn the different ways age can affect your performance in sport. There's more on how your age can influence the types of sports you choose to do on page 96.

Gender, Disability and Performance

In most sports, gender and disability will also affect a participant's performance. Usually (but not always) men and women have separate competitions, and there are different competitions for people of different abilities. If you're doing an Edexcel or WJEC course you can skip this page.

Disability can Also Affect Performance...

1) How much a disability affects performance depends on both the disability and the sport — some disabilities will make particular activities harder to do.

2) Many competitions take disability into account by setting up disability categories. That way people with equivalent disabilities can compete against each other, which makes the competition fair.

...and so can Gender

1) Men and Women have Different Bodies

- Men tend to have larger physiques than women.
- They tend to have bigger hearts and lung capacities — which means they often have naturally higher levels of cardiovascular fitness.
- Men's metabolisms are generally better at supplying energy to their muscles, which means they can usually perform better in physical activities than women.

2) Men are Generally Stronger

Men have bigger muscles, due to higher levels of the hormone testosterone, making them better at activities that rely on strength.

3) Women are Generally More Flexible

This is partly because they've got less muscle.

4) Girls Mature Earlier Than Boys

- Girls usually reach physical maturity at about 16
- Boys aren't usually physically mature until about 20.

Women are generally more flexible.

Remember, gender matters — choose the correct changing room...

Make sure you learn how gender and disability can affect your performance in sport. List the differences between men and women that affect performance. There's more on how gender can influence the types of sports you choose to do on pages 95 and 96.

Somatotypes

Somatotype means the basic shape of your body. There are three main body types you need to know. If you're doing an OCR or WJEC course, you can just ignore the next few pages and skip straight to p42.

Somatotypes are Body Types

1) There are three basic somatotypes — ectomorph, mesomorph and endomorph.

2) Very few people are a perfect example of one of these body types — pretty much everyone is a mixture.

3) You can think of these basic somatotypes as extremes — at the corners of a triangular graph (see below).

REMEMBER
EN**D**OMORPH — **Dumpy**
M**E**SOMORPH — **Muscular**
EC**T**OMORPH — **Thin**

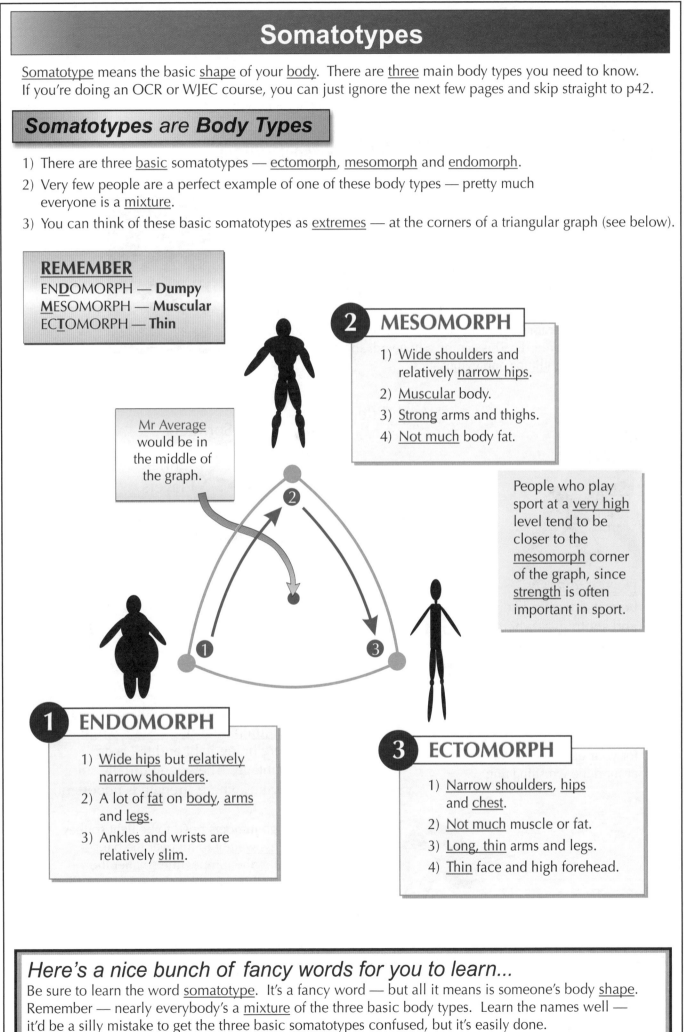

Mr Average would be in the middle of the graph.

2 MESOMORPH
1) Wide shoulders and relatively narrow hips.
2) Muscular body.
3) Strong arms and thighs.
4) Not much body fat.

People who play sport at a very high level tend to be closer to the mesomorph corner of the graph, since strength is often important in sport.

1 ENDOMORPH
1) Wide hips but relatively narrow shoulders.
2) A lot of fat on body, arms and legs.
3) Ankles and wrists are relatively slim.

3 ECTOMORPH
1) Narrow shoulders, hips and chest.
2) Not much muscle or fat.
3) Long, thin arms and legs.
4) Thin face and high forehead.

Here's a nice bunch of fancy words for you to learn...

Be sure to learn the word somatotype. It's a fancy word — but all it means is someone's body shape. Remember — nearly everybody's a mixture of the three basic body types. Learn the names well — it'd be a silly mistake to get the three basic somatotypes confused, but it's easily done.

Somatotypes

Your somatotype can have a big effect on your suitability for a particular sport. Being the right shape is no guarantee of success, but it can really help. As with the previous page, if you're on an OCR or a WJEC course, you can just ignore this page and skip straight on to p42.

Different Somatotypes Suit Different Sports

MESOMORPHS are suited to most types of activity.

1) They're able to build up muscle quickly and easily — which gives them an advantage in any activity where strength is important. E.g. sprinting, tennis, weightlifting...

2) Mesomorphs also have broad shoulders, which make it easier for them to be able to support weight using their upper body. This can be a huge advantage in activities like weightlifting and gymnastics.

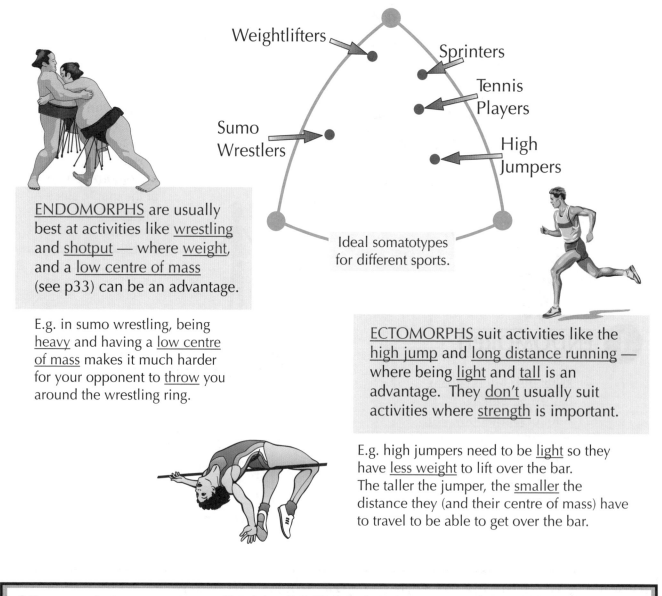

Weightlifters

Sprinters

Tennis Players

Sumo Wrestlers

High Jumpers

Ideal somatotypes for different sports.

ENDOMORPHS are usually best at activities like wrestling and shotput — where weight, and a low centre of mass (see p33) can be an advantage.

E.g. in sumo wrestling, being heavy and having a low centre of mass makes it much harder for your opponent to throw you around the wrestling ring.

ECTOMORPHS suit activities like the high jump and long distance running — where being light and tall is an advantage. They don't usually suit activities where strength is important.

E.g. high jumpers need to be light so they have less weight to lift over the bar. The taller the jumper, the smaller the distance they (and their centre of mass) have to travel to be able to get over the bar.

All somatotypes are suited to tiddlywinks...

Whatever your shape, there'll be a sport out there that you're ideally suited to, giving you the advantage over your opponents. Make sure you know which activities each somatotype is suited to.

Optimum Weight

Everyone's expected and optimum weights are slightly <u>different</u>. If you're doing an Edexcel course, you need to know why they differ and the factors that affect them. Everyone else can skip on to the next page.

Expected and *Optimum Weight* Depend on Many Things...

1) A person's <u>expected weight</u> is (unsurprisingly) the weight you'd <u>expect</u> them to be, based on their height.

2) Your <u>optimum weight</u> is the weight at which you <u>perform</u> at your <u>best</u> at the activities you do.

3) Two people of the <u>same height</u> are likely to have <u>different</u> optimum weights for many reasons:

1) <u>BONE STRUCTURE</u> — some people have a <u>larger</u> <u>bone structure</u> than others. The <u>more bone</u> you have, the <u>higher</u> your optimum weight will be.

2) <u>MUSCLE GIRTH</u> — this is a measurement of the <u>circumference</u> (the distance around) your muscles when they're flexed. Some people naturally have <u>more muscle</u> than others — which means they'll have a <u>larger</u> muscle girth and a <u>higher</u> optimum weight.

3) <u>GENDER</u> — men and women naturally have different body compositions. Men usually have <u>larger bone structures</u> and <u>more muscle</u> than women, so men generally have <u>higher</u> optimum weights.

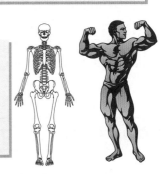

4) <u>ACTIVITY</u> — your optimum weight depends on the <u>activity</u> you want to do. A <u>jockey</u> has a <u>low</u> optimum weight, while a <u>heavyweight boxer</u> has a <u>high</u> optimum weight.

5) <u>AGE</u> — as you get older you tend to <u>lose muscle</u> and your <u>bone density</u> can decrease. So as you age, your optimum weight gets <u>lighter</u>.

Competitive pie eaters have a high expected weight...

So even if you're the same height as someone else, your optimum weight can be very different. Learn the definitions of expected and optimum weight, and the five reasons optimum weight varies.

Weight and Performance

People come in all different shapes, sizes and weights. To be <u>healthy</u>, it's not your actual weight that's the most important factor, it's how much of that weight is <u>fat</u>.

*Being **Overweight** or **Overfat** Affects Performance*

> Being **OVERWEIGHT** means weighing <u>more</u> than is <u>normal</u>.

> **OVERFAT** means having more <u>body fat</u> than you should. Being OBESE means being <u>very overfat</u>.

1) Being overweight <u>doesn't</u> necessarily mean you're <u>unhealthy</u>, e.g. you could just have more <u>muscle</u> than average. Being overweight is usually only <u>harmful</u> when it's caused by being <u>overfat</u> or <u>obese</u>.

2) Being overfat or obese means you're basically carrying <u>extra weight</u> around. It could be due to a <u>poor diet</u> or <u>over-eating</u>. This can mean you get <u>tired</u> more easily, so you might not be able to do <u>high endurance</u> sports, e.g. tennis or long distance running.

3) Being overfat or obese can also <u>limit</u> your <u>flexibility</u> and limb movement. The <u>stress</u> the excess weight puts on the body (especially the heart) can make doing <u>vigorous exercise</u> potentially <u>harmful</u>.

4) Obesity usually has a <u>bad</u> affect on <u>performance</u>, but there are some sports where you need to be obese to be at your <u>optimum weight</u> (e.g. in sumo wrestling).

5) In sport, you can be classed as underweight if you weigh less than you <u>need</u> to for your activity. E.g. being underweight could mean being <u>too light</u> to fight in a particular <u>weight division</u>.

*Being **Underweight** can Affect Performance Too*

> Being **UNDERWEIGHT** means weighing <u>less</u> than is <u>normal</u>, <u>needed</u> or <u>healthy</u>.

Being <u>underweight</u> because of a <u>poor diet</u> or <u>under-eating</u> may mean you don't have <u>enough energy</u> or the <u>muscular endurance</u> to do physical activities for long periods of time.

> <u>Anorexia</u> is an <u>eating disorder</u> where sufferers believe they're fat and <u>starve</u> themselves to lose weight. Without sufficient nutrients in their diet, sufferers will feel <u>extremely tired</u>, their muscles will start to <u>waste away</u> and their <u>bones weaken</u> — doing any physical activity can become extremely difficult.

So there'll be no sumo marathon then...

Now we're getting on to the heavyweight subjects (ho ho ho...). Keep going over this page until you know how weight can affect your performance, and all the <u>underweight</u> and <u>overweight</u> stuff too.

Warm-Up and Worked Exam Questions

Worked Exam Questions

You know the drill by now — look through the worked examples, then have a bash at the questions yourself on the next page.

1 Give **one** characteristic feature of body shape for each of the following somatotypes.

a) Endomorph *Wide hips*

b) Mesomorph *Muscular*

c) Ectomorph *Thin*

There are other possible answers you could give.

(3 marks)

2 Suggest a physical activity which is suited to each somatotype below. Give **one** reason why a person with that body type would have an advantage in the named activity.

a) Mesomorph

Tennis. Being strong will mean they can hit the tennis ball with more force, making it travel faster, so it's more difficult to return.

(2 marks)

b) Endomorph

Sumo wresting. Having a high weight and a lower centre of mass makes it more difficult for an opponent to throw the participant.

(2 marks)

3 What is meant by the term 'obese'? Name **one** possible cause of obesity.

Being very over fat — having much more body fat than you should. You can become obese by over-eating.

(2 marks)

Exam Questions

1   Which of the following sports would an endomorph be particularly suited to?

    A   Golf

    B   Tennis

    C   Shotput

    D   High jump

(1 mark)

2   Give **three** physical factors that make it inappropriate for men and women to compete against each other in most sports.

....

....

....

(3 marks)

3   Tim is a professional wrestler. His optimum weight is higher than his expected weight.

    a)   Describe the difference between expected weight and optimum weight.

....

....

....

(2 marks)

    b)   Suggest **one** reason why being heavier than his expected weight is an advantage for Tim in wrestling.

....

....

(1 mark)

4   Age affects performance in sport. Most professional footballers are in their twenties, whereas many professional golfers are much older than this. Suggest possible reasons for this difference.

....

....

....

....

(4 marks)

Diet and Nutrition

"You are what you eat," people sometimes say — that's how <u>vital</u> this subject is. It's very important to know about different foods, <u>what</u> they contain, and <u>why</u> we need to eat them.

You Need to Eat a **Balanced Diet** to be **Healthy**

1) Eating a balanced diet is an <u>important</u> part of a healthy, active lifestyle.

2) What makes up a balanced diet is slightly <u>different</u> for everyone. E.g. if you exercise loads, you'll need to eat more high energy foods than someone who doesn't.

> A **balanced diet** contains the <u>best ratio</u> of nutrients to match your lifestyle.

3) If you <u>don't</u> eat a balanced diet, not only could you be <u>physically unable</u> to do the activities you want to, but you might actually be <u>damaging</u> your body, e.g. if you eat a lot of <u>fatty foods</u>, you might end up with <u>high blood pressure</u>, which increases the risk of <u>heart disease</u> and <u>strokes</u>.

You Need **More of Some** Nutrients **Than Others**

There are <u>two</u> main groups of nutrients your body needs:
<u>Macro nutrients</u> — nutrients your body needs in <u>large</u> amounts.
<u>Micro nutrients</u> — nutrients your body still needs, but in <u>smaller</u> amounts.

MACRO NUTRIENTS:
1) Proteins
2) Carbohydrates
3) Fats

MICRO NUTRIENTS:
1) Vitamins
2) Minerals

WATER AND DIETARY FIBRE

On top of these, you also need plenty of <u>water</u> and <u>dietary fibre</u> in your diet to be healthy. The best way to get all of these nutrients is to eat a <u>varied</u> diet with plenty of <u>fruit</u> and <u>vegetables</u>, but not too much <u>fat</u>.

Carbohydrates, **Fats** and **Proteins** are **Macro Nutrients**

Carbohydrates, fats and proteins are <u>macro nutrients</u> — they make up the bulk of your food. They provide you with <u>energy</u> and help you <u>grow</u>.

CARBOHYDRATES

1) Carbohydrates are the main source of <u>energy</u> for the body.

2) You can get <u>simple</u> ones, e.g. sugar, and <u>complex</u> ones, e.g. starch.

3) Whenever you eat carbohydrates, some will get <u>used</u> by the body <u>straight away</u>.

4) The rest gets <u>stored</u> in the liver and muscles ready for when it's needed.

PROTEINS

1) Proteins help the body <u>grow</u> and <u>repair itself</u>.

2) They're made from molecules called <u>amino acids</u> — your body can make most amino acids but some you have to get from food.

This pie chart shows about how much of each nutrient you should eat.

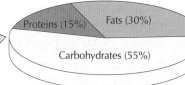
Proteins (15%) Fats (30%) Carbohydrates (55%)

FATS

1) Fats are made from molecules called <u>fatty acids</u> and <u>glycerol</u>.

2) They provide <u>energy</u> for the body but they're also really important for helping keep the <u>body warm</u> and <u>protecting organs</u>. There are also some <u>vitamins</u> that the body can <u>only</u> absorb using fats.

3) Some fats are turned into <u>cholesterol</u> by the <u>liver</u>. Cholesterol can be transported in <u>high</u> or <u>low</u> density lipoproteins (<u>HDLs</u> and <u>LDLs</u>). Having <u>too much LDL</u> cholesterol increases the risk of <u>heart attacks</u> and <u>strokes</u>. Having high levels of <u>HDLs</u> is <u>good</u>, as it helps the body get rid of excess cholesterol.

Diet and Nutrition

Micro nutrients are just as important as macro nutrients — you just need smaller amounts of them.

You need Small Amounts of Vitamins and Minerals

VITAMINS

1) Vitamins help keep your bones, teeth and skin healthy.

2) They're also needed for many of the body's chemical reactions.

With a properly balanced diet, you don't need vitamin supplements.

FAT-SOLUBLE VITAMINS — can be stored in the body.

E.g. Vitamin A — needed for your growth and vision, and can be found in vegetables, eggs and liver.
Vitamin D — needed for strong bones, so you don't get bone-softening diseases like osteoporosis (see p24). Vitamin D can be made by the skin in sunshine, but it's also found in milk, fish, liver and eggs.

WATER-SOLUBLE VITAMINS — can't be stored, so you need to eat them regularly.

E.g. Vitamin C — good for your skin and the stuff that holds your body tissues together. Without it, your body tissues can't form properly and you get a nasty disease called scurvy. Vitamin C is found in fruit and veg — especially citrus fruits like oranges and lemons.

MINERALS

1) These are needed for healthy bones and teeth, and to build other tissues.

2) Minerals help in various chemical reactions in the body.

E.g. Calcium is needed for strong bones and teeth, and also for muscle contractions (see p14). There's lots in green vegetables, milk, cheese and some fish.

Iron is needed for making red blood cells (see p11). Without it your blood can't carry much oxygen. There's tons in liver, beans and green vegetables.

Water and Dietary Fibre are Just as Important

WATER

1) Water's needed in loads of chemical reactions in the body. It's also lost in your breath, sweat, urine and faeces.

2) If you don't drink enough to replace what your body uses or loses you'll become dehydrated, and you won't perform as well.

3) If you drink more than you need, your kidneys will produce more urine to get rid of the excess.

DIETARY FIBRE

1) You need fibre to keep your digestive system working properly.

2) There's lots of fibre in fruit and vegetables — another good reason to eat loads of them.

Your Diet can help Improve your Performance

1) Most athletes plan their diets to help improve their performance — e.g. runners will eat lots of carbohydrates before an event, while weightlifters eat lots of protein to build up their muscles.

2) When you eat is also important — you should eat lots of carbohydrates before exercising, but don't eat anything immediately before, during or immediately after exercising (you should drink lots of water though).

3) Thanks to blood shunting (see p22) your digestive system has a limited blood supply when you exercise. Any food in your digestive system won't be able to be digested properly, so you're more likely to feel sick.

Recreational Drugs

Recreational drugs (i.e. drugs people take for enjoyment) can have a negative effect on your health and can affect your performance in sports. If you're doing a WJEC or AQA course, you can just skip this page.

Alcohol Damages your Performance

Although alcohol is legal, it's still a drug and can affect your performance badly.

1) It affects your coordination, speech and judgement, so you're more likely to hurt yourself. You're also less likely to be able to do things accurately — like shoot in football or return the ball in tennis.
2) It slows your reactions, whether it's to a starter gun in a race or a pass in netball.
3) It makes your muscles get tired more quickly, so you can't exercise for as long.
4) It increases your blood pressure — the more you drink, the higher it gets.
5) Eventually it damages your liver, kidneys, heart, muscles, brain, and the digestive and immune systems.

Small amounts of alcohol don't do too much harm, but drinking before you do sports can be dangerous — you're more likely to have an accident or hurt others. If you want to have a healthy, active lifestyle and do well in sports, it's best to only drink in moderation (or not at all).

Tobacco is Legal but Harmful

Tobacco is another legal drug, but it's really bad for you.
Every cigarette damages your body and affects your performance in sports.

1) Smoking causes nose, throat and chest irritations.
2) It makes you short of breath, so you find it harder to exercise.
3) Smoking and nicotine cause a temporary rise in blood pressure.
4) It damages your respiratory system (see below) and your cardiovascular system (see p19 and 22). Smoking increases the risk of developing heart disease, cancer, bronchitis, and other diseases.

For a healthy, active lifestyle it's best to avoid smoking altogether.

Smoking Clogs Up the Alveoli

1) Smoking has a really bad effect on your respiratory system.
2) Cigarette smoke contains tar, which clogs up the alveoli and makes it harder for gas exchange to take place. Eventually the alveoli will collapse and stop working.
3) Even if the tar is removed and the alveoli are repaired, they'll never be as efficient as they were.
4) Cigarette smoke also contains the addictive drug and poison nicotine. Nicotine causes the blood vessels in the lungs to tighten, which slows the blood flow in the lungs making the gas exchange in the alveoli less efficient.

Doesn't sound like fun to me...

Some people use alcohol and tobacco to calm their nerves and improve their performance — some darts players drink alcohol whilst they play to help get them 'in the zone'. But, alcohol affects your judgement, coordination and reactions — so it usually has a negative effect your performance.

Performance-Enhancing Drugs

Some people cheat by taking <u>drugs</u>. Drugs can sometimes make them <u>perform</u> better, but there are <u>risks</u> and nasty side effects... If you're doing an AQA course, you don't need to know this page.

Many *Drugs* can *Improve Performance*

Some athletes use drugs to <u>improve</u> their performance. The use of these drugs in sport is usually <u>banned</u>, and they usually have <u>nasty side effects</u>. Unfortunately, some athletes still <u>break the rules</u> by taking them anyway — even with the <u>risks</u>. (Breaking the rules like this is sometimes called <u>deviance</u>.)

These are the drugs you need to know about:

REMEMBER — BAD SNaP	
B	— Beta blockers
A	— Anabolic steroids
D	— Diuretics
S	— Stimulants
Na	— Narcotic analgesics
P	— Peptide hormones

BETA BLOCKERS

- Are drugs that <u>control</u> heart rate.
- They <u>lower the heart rate</u>, <u>steady shaking hands</u>, and have a <u>calming</u>, <u>relaxing</u> effect.

But...

- They can cause <u>low blood pressure</u>, <u>cramp</u> and <u>heart failure</u>.

STIMULANTS

- Affect the <u>central nervous system</u> (the bits of your brain and spine that control your <u>reactions</u>).
- They can <u>increase mental</u> and <u>physical alertness</u>.

But...

- They can lead to <u>high blood pressure</u>, <u>heart</u> and <u>liver problems</u>, and <u>strokes</u>.
- They're <u>addictive</u>.

ANABOLIC STEROIDS

- Mimic the male sex hormone <u>testosterone</u>.
- Testosterone <u>increases</u> your <u>bone</u> and <u>muscle growth</u> (so you can get bigger and stronger). It can also make you more <u>aggressive</u>.

But...

- They cause <u>high blood pressure</u>, <u>heart disease</u>, <u>infertility</u> and <u>cancer</u>.
- Women may grow <u>facial</u> and <u>body hair</u>, and their voice may <u>deepen</u>.

NARCOTIC ANALGESICS

- <u>Kill pain</u> — so injuries and fatigue don't affect performance so much.

But...

- They're <u>addictive</u>, with unpleasant <u>withdrawal symptoms</u>.
- Feeling less pain can make an athlete train <u>too hard</u>.
- They can lead to <u>constipation</u> and <u>low blood pressure</u>.

DIURETICS

- Increase the amount you <u>urinate</u>, causing <u>weight loss</u> — important if you're competing in a certain <u>weight division</u>.
- Can <u>mask traces</u> of other drugs in the body.

But...

- They can cause <u>cramp</u> and <u>dehydration</u>.

PEPTIDE HORMONES

- Cause the production of other hormones — <u>similar</u> to anabolic steroids.
- <u>EPO</u> (Erythropoietin) is a peptide hormone that causes the body to produce more red blood cells.

But...

- They can cause <u>strokes</u> and <u>abnormal growth</u>.

Blood Doping *is Banned*

You can improve your performance by <u>increasing</u> the number of <u>red blood cells</u> in your bloodstream to increase the <u>oxygen supply</u> to your muscles.

You can do this by <u>altitude training</u> (see p66) or <u>cheat</u> and get the same effect by <u>blood doping</u>.

Blood doping can be done in different ways.

1) Before a competition an athlete can be <u>injected</u> with red blood cells.
   Possible side effects of injecting red blood cells include <u>allergic reactions</u>, <u>kidney damage</u> and <u>blocked capillaries</u> or, if the blood is from someone else, catching <u>viruses</u> such as HIV.

2) Athletes can also take <u>EPO</u> to increase their red blood cell count (see peptide hormones above).

Warm-Up and Worked Exam Questions

Warm-Up Questions

1) What is the definition of a balanced diet?
2) How do the two different types of cholesterol (LDL and HDL) affect the body?
3) Explain the effect that smoking has on gas exchange in the lungs.
4) What effect does alcohol have on blood pressure?
5) Why do some athletes risk taking banned drugs?
6) Name two legal drugs that can negatively affect performance in sport.
7) Name three performance-enhancing drugs.

Worked Exam Questions

Take a look over these examples, then try some exam-style questions yourself.

1   This question is about diet and nutrition.

a)   List **two** nutrients that provide the body with energy.

Carbohydrates and fats.

(2 marks)

b)   Describe why the following substances are necessary in a person's diet:

i) Protein

For repair of tissues and growth.

ii) Vitamins and minerals

You could also say that they help keep your teeth, skin and other tissues healthy, and help chemical reactions that happen in the body.

To ensure healthy bones.

iii) Fibre

To keep the digestive system functioning properly.

(3 marks)

2   Some athletes take anabolic steroids to improve their performance.

a)   Explain how steroids can improve performance.

They help to build up muscle strength and size, which can improve performance in activities where strength is important, e.g. boxing.

(2 marks)

b)   Give **two** possible negative side effects of taking steroids.

Infertility and high blood pressure.

You could also put heart disease, cancer, facial and body hair on women, or a deeper voice in women.

(2 marks)

Exam Questions

1   Which of the following nutrients is **not** a macro nutrient?

   A   Protein

   B   Fat

   C   Fibre

   D   Carbohydrate

(1 mark)

2   Chris and Val are both serious athletes. Chris is a weightlifter and Val is a marathon runner. They have both adapted their diets to improve their performance.
Suggest how each person may have adapted their diet, and how this change might help improve their performance.

....

....

....

(4 marks)

3   Complete the table below to identify and describe the effects of some performance-enhancing drugs.

Name of Drug	Reason drug is taken	Side Effect
Stimulants		high blood pressure
	kill pain so athlete can train for longer/harder	constipation
EPO / Peptide hormones		abnormal growth
Diuretics	weight loss caused by frequent urination	
Beta blockers		addiction

(5 marks)

4   Explain what is meant by the term 'blood doping' and why an athlete might risk doing it.

....

....

....

....

(4 marks)

Revision Summary — Section Three

That's it then — the end of another section. There's lots in it, but it's all stuff you need to know for the exam. You'll need to learn all the info about fitness — what it is and how things like diet, age, drugs and so on can affect it. But don't panic — all you need to do is learn the facts, and then the exam will be easy. To test how much you know, and how much you still need to revise, try these questions — and keep revising until you know all the answers.

1) Name the three types of macro nutrient. Name the two types of micro nutrient.
2) As well as macro and micro nutrients, what two other things do you need for a balanced diet?
3) About what percentage of protein should you have in your diet?
4) Name two fat-soluble vitamins.
5) Name a food that is high in vitamin C.
6) What is calcium needed for?
7) Explain why water and dietary fibre are important in a balanced diet.
8) Is cardiovascular fitness a part of health-related fitness or skill-related fitness?
9) Which two organs are involved in cardiovascular fitness?
10) Describe fast twitch and slow twitch fibres.
11) Define 'flexibility'.
12) Name the three things that make up your body composition.
13) Name and describe the three kinds of strength.
14) Define 'speed'.
15) What is reaction time?
16) Describe 'power'.
17) What do the letters stand for in the ABC of skill-related fitness?
18) Give four ways age can affect your performance in sport.
19) Give three ways gender can affect your performance in sport.
20) Name the three basic somatotypes and write down their main characteristics.
21) For each somatotype, write down one sport it's suited to.
22) Name three factors that affect your optimum weight.
23) Describe what the terms 'underweight' and 'overweight' mean.
24) What is obesity? What is anorexia?
25) Name two recreational drugs and describe the effects they can have.
26) What do beta blockers do?
27) What are the side effects of stimulants?
28) Name two other performance-enhancing drugs.
29) Describe blood doping.
30) Name three possible side effects of blood doping.

PAR-Q and Personal Readiness

If you want to try a new physical activity, make sure it's <u>appropriate</u> for you — fill in a <u>PAR-Q</u> and have some <u>health checks</u> to make sure you're fit enough to do it. Otherwise you might hurt yourself...

Choose an Activity That's *Appropriate* for *You*

It's <u>important</u> to choose an activity that you're <u>fit enough</u> to <u>start</u> and that is <u>suitable</u> for you.
What you choose might depend on a few things:

FITNESS LEVELS

You should start at a <u>level</u> that's <u>right for you</u>. It's probably not a good idea to try and run a marathon if you're only used to walking around the shops.

PHYSICAL MATURITY

Someone who's <u>still growing</u> might not have the <u>strength</u> or <u>endurance</u> for high intensity sports, and could permanently <u>injure</u> themselves by doing them.

AGE

As you get older your body becomes <u>weaker</u>, so older people might prefer <u>non-contact</u> sports instead of sports like rugby or boxing, where it's more <u>likely</u> they will get <u>injured</u>.

PAR-Q — *Physical Activity Readiness Questionnaire*

Once you've decided on an activity, you need to make sure you're <u>physically ready</u> and <u>able</u> to do it.

1) <u>Increasing</u> the amount of physical activity you do is normally a safe thing to do — but if you have an <u>injury</u> or <u>physical problem</u> it could damage your health.

2) <u>PAR-Qs</u> are questionnaires made up of 'yes or no' questions, designed to <u>assess</u> your <u>personal readiness</u> (whether it's <u>safe</u> for you) to increase your physical activity.

3) If you answer <u>no</u> to all of the questions, you can be <u>fairly</u> sure it's safe for you to increase your physical activity.

4) If you answer <u>yes</u> to any of the questions, you need to visit your <u>doctor</u> to make sure it's safe first.

PAR-Q	Yes	No
1) Have you ever experienced any chest pain while doing physical activity?	☐	☐
2) Have you ever been diagnosed with a heart problem?	☐	☐
3) Are you currently being prescribed any medication?	☐	☐
4) Do you have a joint problem that may be made worse by physical activity?	☐	☐

PAR-Qs can lessen your risk of injury...

Being fit is really important, but there's no point trying to improve your fitness if you're just going to end up doing more harm than good. By choosing a suitable activity for your fitness level and age, and filling in a PAR-Q before you start doing the activity, you reduce your chance of getting injured.

Health Screening

Health screening is another way to assess your personal readiness for starting an activity.

Health Screening Makes Sure You're in Tip Top Condition

Here are the health checks and tests you need to know:

Measuring Blood Pressure

1) Exercise can put a lot of stress on the body.

2) High or low blood pressure could indicate a problem with your heart or cardiovascular system (see page 19) — which could make it dangerous to start doing vigorous exercise.

Checking Lifestyle and Family History

1) Looking at your lifestyle and checking your family medical history might give clues about any health problems you might suffer.

2) You're more likely to suffer from some things if your parents or grandparents had them, e.g. high blood pressure or heart disease.

Measuring Body Mass Index (BMI)

1) BMI is a way of working out if you're at a healthy weight (see page 30).

2) But, it only takes into account your height and not your age or fitness.

Measuring Resting Heart Rate

1) Resting heart rate is a good measure of cardiovascular fitness.

2) The lower your resting heart rate, the better your cardiovascular system is (see page 24).

With all tests, you should check:

1) its validity — does it test what it should?

2) its reliability — does it give repeatable, consistent results?

E.g. BMI is a very reliable test — it'll give you exactly the same result for the same height and weight each time. It might not be a very valid test for everyone though, e.g. being healthy but having a lot of muscle could give a BMI indicating an unhealthy weight.

Health checks check your health...

As well as assessing your personal readiness for an activity, having health checks can also help you to find out about any possible health problems before they become an issue. Make sure you know all the health checks and tests on this page, and learn what 'validity' and 'reliability' mean.

Fitness Testing

You should <u>test</u> your fitness <u>before</u> you start training. That way you'll be able to see how you're <u>improving</u> when you test it again.

*There are Some **Simple** Ways to **Monitor Fitness***

Heart Rate Monitors

These <u>monitor</u> your <u>heart rate</u>.
You can see how <u>strenuous</u> an activity is by measuring how much your heart rate goes <u>up</u>.

Pedometers

These record the <u>number of steps</u> you take. They can be used to work out how many calories you've burnt.

Diary Keeping

This is an easy way of <u>recording</u> the amount of activity that you do. It's good for <u>monitoring improvements</u> in your fitness.

*You Need to Know **Tests** for **Cardiovascular Endurance***

COOPER'S 12-MINUTE RUN TEST

1) <u>Jog</u> to warm up.
2) Then <u>run</u> around a track as many times as you can in 12 minutes.
3) The further you can run, the fitter you are.

Remember to think about how <u>valid</u> and <u>reliable</u> each test is.

TREADMILL TEST

1) Treadmill tests usually test <u>how long</u> you can run for.
2) Start walking with the treadmill on a slow/flat setting, then gradually increase the <u>slope</u> and/or the <u>speed</u>.
3) The <u>longer</u> you can run for, the <u>fitter</u> you are.

MULTI-STAGE FITNESS TEST (MSFT)

1) A recording of a series of <u>timed bleeps</u> is played.
2) You have to run 'shuttles' between 2 lines, 20 metres apart, starting on the first bleep.
3) Your foot must be <u>on</u> or <u>over</u> the next line when the next bleep sounds.
4) After about a minute the time between bleeps gets <u>shorter</u>, so you have to <u>run</u> faster.
5) If you miss a bleep you are allowed two further bleeps to catch up. If you miss <u>three</u> bleeps in a row, the <u>level</u> and <u>number</u> of shuttles completed are noted as your final score.

HARVARD STEP TEST

1) Using a 45 cm step, do <u>30 step-ups a minute</u> for 5 minutes. (Or if you have to go slower, keep going for <u>20 seconds</u> after you <u>begin</u> to slow down, then stop.)
2) <u>Rest</u> for 1 minute, then take your pulse for 15 seconds — multiply this by 4 to get your heart rate.

$$\frac{\text{length of exercise in seconds} \times 100}{5.5 \times \text{pulse count}}$$

3) Use this <u>formula</u> to work out your score — the higher your score, the fitter you are.

4) There are different versions of the Harvard step test so check the details (height of the step, rest time etc.) before comparing results.

Fitness testing lets you monitor your progress...

Make sure you know the different ways to monitor fitness and how to test cardiovascular endurance.

Fitness Testing

There are tests for other components of <u>health-related fitness</u> too.

You need to know these tests for *Health-Related Fitness*

Body Composition

CALLIPERS

1) <u>Skin fold callipers</u> are used to pinch your <u>skin</u> and <u>underlying fat</u> — you can plug these measurements into an equation to estimate your <u>body fat percentage</u>.

2) To get a good estimate, you have to be pinched in the <u>right way</u>.

3) The percentage of your total body fat stored under the skin depends on factors like <u>age</u> and <u>gender</u>. You can use <u>different equations</u> to take this into account and make your estimate more <u>accurate</u>.

BODY DENSITY TEST

In a <u>body density test</u>, you weigh yourself on <u>land</u> and <u>underwater</u>. Then, you can use the two measurements and some clever maths, to work out your body density and <u>percentage body fat</u>.

Muscular Endurance

SIT-UPS AND PRESS-UPS

To test the <u>endurance</u> of different muscles, see <u>how many times</u> you can do an exercise — e.g. abdominal curls (sit-ups) or press-ups.

Muscular Strength

HAND GRIP TEST

This kind of <u>dynamometer</u> measures <u>hand</u> and <u>forearm strength</u>. Just grip as hard as you can...

Flexibility

SIT AND REACH TEST

This measures <u>flexibility</u> in the <u>back</u> and <u>lower hamstrings</u>.

1) Sit on the floor with your legs pointing <u>straight</u> out in front of you.

2) Push a ruler, placed on a box, as far <u>forwards</u> as you can with your fingers — keeping your legs <u>straight</u> all the time.

ruler

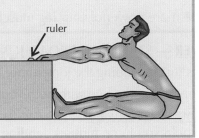

Make sure you have a good grip of these tests...

Make sure you know what aspect of health-related fitness each test is measuring. You can use these tests to work out what aspects of fitness you need to improve. You can also use them to help create an exercise or training programme that will suit a person's needs and fitness levels.

Fitness Testing

You've got to know how to test the components of <u>skill-related fitness</u> too. Here's the info...

*You can **Test** Your **Agility**, **Balance** and **Coordination**...*

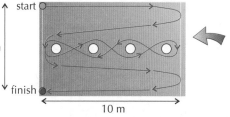

5 m

start

finish

10 m

AGILITY — ILLINOIS AGILITY RUN TEST

1) Set out a course using cones.

2) Start <u>lying face down</u> at the start cone. When the start whistle blows, run around the circuit as fast as you can.

3) The course is set up so you have to constantly <u>change direction</u>.

4) The <u>more agile</u> you are, the <u>quicker</u> you'll be able to complete the course.

BALANCE — THE STANDING STORK TEST

Stand on your best leg with your other foot touching your knee and your hands on your hips. The heel of the foot you are standing on should be <u>off the floor</u>. Time how long you can stand there. <u>Wobbling</u>'s allowed, but no moving your feet or hands. Take the <u>best of three</u> times.

COORDINATION — ALTERNATE HAND THROW

1) For this you need to stand in front of a <u>wall</u>.

2) <u>Throw</u> a ball from your <u>right</u> hand against a wall and <u>catch</u> it your <u>left</u> — then throw it from your left hand back against the wall and catch it in your right.

3) The <u>more</u> throws and catches you can do in 30 seconds, the <u>better</u> your <u>coordination</u>.

COORDINATION — 3-BALL JUGGLE

To be able to juggle, you need to be <u>coordinated</u>. The better your coordination, the <u>longer</u> you should be able to juggle for.

*...as well as Your **Speed**, **Reactions** and **Power***

REACTIONS — THE RULER DROP TEST

1) Get a friend to hold a ruler <u>vertically</u> between your thumb and first finger. The <u>0 cm</u> mark on the ruler should be <u>in line</u> with the <u>top of your thumb</u>.

2) Your friend drops the ruler — you have to try and catch it <u>as soon as you see it drop</u>.

3) Read off the distance the ruler fell before you managed to catch it. The <u>slower</u> your reactions, the longer it takes you to catch the ruler, so the further up the ruler you'll catch it.

POWER — SARGENT/VERTICAL JUMP TEST

1) Put chalk on your finger tips and stand <u>side-on</u> to a wall.

2) Raise the arm that's nearest the wall and mark the <u>highest point</u> you can reach.

3) Still standing side-on to the wall, <u>jump</u> and <u>mark the wall</u> as high up as you can.

4) The more <u>powerful</u> your leg muscles are, the larger the <u>distance between</u> your first and second mark.

POWER — STANDING BROAD JUMP TEST

This is just like doing the long jump, but from a <u>standing start</u>.

1) Stand behind a line with both your feet next to each other.

2) <u>Jump</u> as far <u>forward</u> as you can (you can swing your arms to help you jump further), <u>landing on both feet</u>.

3) How far you jump depends on the <u>power</u> your leg muscles can produce. The greater the power, the further you jump.

SPEED — 30 M/50 M SPRINT TEST

Simply time how long it takes you to <u>run 30</u> or <u>50 m</u>.

Here's another test for you...

Write down all the ways to test <u>agility</u>, <u>balance</u>, <u>coordination</u>, <u>speed</u>, <u>reactions</u> and <u>power</u>...

Warm-Up and Worked Exam Questions

Warm-Up Questions

1) Explain why your physical maturity may limit the activities which are suitable for you to do.
2) What does 'PAR-Q' stand for?
3) Name two health checks that might be performed as part of health screening.
4) List three tests for cardiovascular endurance.
5) Describe two tests that could be used to calculate body composition.
6) Name a test for speed.
7) Why might BMI not always be a good indicator of physical well-being?

Worked Exam Questions

Here we go again, a worked exam question followed by you know what — yup, having a go yourself.

1   A coach wants to assess the fitness of a rugby player before he allows him to join his team.

a)   The coach makes the player fill in a PAR-Q to assess his personal readiness. Explain why assessing personal readiness before starting an activity is important.

It helps you to decide whether it is safe for you to increase your

level of physical activity.

(1 mark)

b)   Complete the table below.

i) State **two** aspects of fitness that are needed to perform well in rugby.

ii) Name **one** appropriate test for each aspect of fitness named in part i).

i) Aspect of Fitness	ii) Fitness Test
Cardiovascular fitness	Multi-stage fitness test
Agility	Illinois agility run test

(4 marks)

c)   Describe the procedure for carrying out **one** test named in part a).

Don't forget to state which fitness test you have chosen.

In the multi-stage fitness test, a series of timed beeps is played. You run between two lines 20 metres apart. Your foot must be on or over the line on the beeps. Miss three beeps in a row and your score is noted. The higher the score the higher the fitness.

This is worth three marks, so make sure that you give three relevant points.

(3 marks)

Exam Questions

1   Which of the following could be used to test power?

    A   Ruler drop test

    B   Standing stork test

    C   Standing broad jump test

    D   Harvard step test

(1 mark)

2   Which of the following fitness tests is the **least** suitable test for cardiovascular fitness.

    A   Treadmill test

    B   Multi-stage fitness test

    C   Coopers 12 minute run

    D   30 m sprint test

(1 mark)

3   Charlene is a good club-level gymnast. She prefers to work on the beam.

    a)   Name **two** components of fitness that she needs to work on the beam.

        ....

(2 marks)

    b)   For **one** of these components of fitness, suggest a suitable test she could use to measure it and describe the procedure for carrying out this test.

        ....

        ....

        ....

(3 marks)

4   You have been asked to design a training programme for a karate student who wants to improve their flexibility, reactions and muscular endurance. Name and describe **two** fitness tests that should be carried out before a training programme is created.

    Test 1 ....

    ....

    ....

    Test 2 ....

    ....

    ....

(6 marks)

Training Sessions

Training's not just about running for as long as possible, or lifting the heaviest weights you can. There's much more to it than that — and you'll probably be asked about it in the exam, so get reading.

Train to Improve Your Health, Fitness or Performance

1) To improve your health, fitness or performance, you should follow a Personal Exercise Programme (PEP).
2) A PEP is a training programme designed to improve whatever you want it to improve
— it could be your general health and fitness, or a particular skill.

> **TRAINING** — a programme designed to improve your performance, physical fitness, or skills (including motor skills).

A motor skill is a learned set of movements that make up a smooth, efficient action e.g. walking, or a tennis serve.

3) A PEP needs to be interesting and must suit the person it's for — so you've got to find out about them. Which means asking them some questions like: What type of exercise do you like? How fit are you now? There's more about creating a PEP on page 68.

SPORT — The Five Principles of Training

To get the most from your training you should follow the principles of SPORT.

S ➡ **SPECIFICITY / INDIVIDUAL NEEDS** — Every person will need a different training programme suited to them and the sport they want to do.

1) Train the parts of the body that are specific to that sport — there's no point making a weightlifter run 10 miles a day — it won't improve their weightlifting.
2) Training needs to be done at the right level for the individual — if someone's dead unfit, don't start them with a 5-mile swim.

P ➡ **PROGRESSION** — Steadily increase the amount of training that's done. But only when the body has adapted to the previous training, so you avoid injury.

O ➡ **OVERLOAD** — You've got to make your body work harder than it normally would. Overload is the only way to get fitter. You can overload by increasing the frequency, intensity, or the duration of the training (see next page).

R ➡ **REVERSIBILITY** — any fitness improvement or body adaptation caused by training will gradually reverse and be lost when you stop training. It takes much longer to gain fitness than to lose fitness, which isn't ideal.

The 'R' stands for 'rest and recovery' in the Edexcel courses.

T ➡ **TEDIUM** — The time you spend training needs to be interesting as well as useful. You need to do different things in each session — otherwise you'll get bored and never want to do any training at all.

You Need to Rest and Recover After Training

1) You also need to allow time for your body to repair itself and recover after vigorous exercise.

> **REST** and **RECOVERY**: Recovery is the time needed for your body to repair any damage caused by physical activity. Rest is the amount of time you allow your body to recover.

2) You need to rest until your body has fully recovered, or you'll just end up injuring yourself.
3) But, if you rest for too long, reversibility will mean you'll lose all the benefits of doing the training.
4) If you get injured, not only have you got to wait for your injury to heal, but, thanks to reversibility, your fitness will start to decrease while you do.

Training Sessions

The best training programmes aren't just thrown together — they have to be carefully <u>planned</u>.

Training Programmes can be Planned using FITT

Frequency, intensity and time are all part of making sure you <u>overload</u> while you're training.

F = FREQUENCY of activity — how <u>often</u> you should exercise.

E.g. if you just want to stay healthy you should exercise for at least 20 minutes three to five times a week. If you do a hard workout you should give your body at least <u>24 hours rest</u> before you exercise again.

I = INTENSITY of activity — how <u>hard</u> you should exercise.

E.g. if you wanted to <u>lose weight</u> you should raise your <u>heart rate</u> to about 75% of your maximum safe heart rate (see page 69) for 20 minutes or more.

T = TIME spent on activity — how <u>long</u> you should exercise.

Training sessions to improve <u>cardiovascular fitness</u> tend to last for <u>20 minutes</u> or longer. <u>Strength</u> training sessions are generally shorter and less sustained.

T = TYPE of activity — <u>what exercises</u> you should use.

It can be good to <u>vary</u> training sessions to stop you tiring and getting bored of the same old workout. In aerobic training this is called <u>cross-training</u> — a different exercise (e.g. cycling instead of running) is used to <u>increase fitness</u>, but <u>without over-stressing</u> the tissues and joints used in your main activity.

Eventually your body will <u>adapt</u> to the training — you'll get <u>fitter</u>, and your performance and competence will <u>improve</u>. All training programmes need to be <u>constantly monitored</u> to make sure that the activities are still producing <u>overload</u>. As you get fitter your PEP will need to <u>change</u> to <u>keep</u> improving your fitness.

Always Warm-Up First and Cool-Down Afterwards

<u>All</u> exercise and training sessions should be made up of a <u>warm-up</u>, a <u>main activity</u>, and a <u>cool-down</u>.

WARM-UP
Gets your body ready for exercise.

1) Increases <u>blood flow</u> to the muscles — so they can do the work later on in the training.
2) Stretches the <u>muscles</u>, moves the <u>joints</u> and increases flexibility — so you're ready for the work and less likely to <u>injure</u> yourself.
3) Helps to improve the <u>strength</u> and <u>speed</u> of muscle contractions.
4) Concentrates the <u>mind</u> on the training.

COOL-DOWN
Gets your body back to normal.

1) Helps replace the <u>oxygen</u> in your muscles, and so gets rid of any <u>lactic acid</u> and other waste products.
2) Helps <u>prevent injuries</u> and <u>soreness</u> the following day.

A Training Plan Should Suit the Activity

1) Your training should <u>match</u> the type of activity or component of fitness you want to improve.
2) If you want to be good at an <u>aerobic activity</u> like <u>long distance running</u> — you should do a lot of aerobic activity as part of your training.
3) For <u>anaerobic activities</u> like <u>sprinting</u>, you need to do <u>anaerobic training</u> so your muscles are able to <u>cope with</u> the lactic acid build up and get better at <u>getting rid</u> of it.
4) Lots of activities are a <u>mixture</u> of aerobic and anaerobic activity, so a training plan for these sorts of activities will have a bit of both types of training in it.

Warm-Up and Worked Exam Questions

Warm-Up Questions

1) What must you do after every training session?
2) What do the initials SPORT stand for?
3) What is a PEP?
4) Why is it important to allow time for rest and recovery between exercise sessions?
5) What type of activity should a tennis player do in training — aerobic, anaerobic or both?

Worked Exam Questions

Work through these exam questions carefully, making sure you understand them,
then try the practice questions on the next page.

1   James is an elite performer. At the beginning of each training session he spends
10 minutes warming up.

    a)   What are the benefits of a warm-up?

It focuses the mind and increases blood flow to the muscles.

It also stretches the muscles, helping to increase the range

of movement.

Check the number of marks before
answering a question — it's a good guide
to how much detail you need to go into.

(3 marks)

    b)   Give an example of what could happen to James if he doesn't warm up.

He could injure himself.

(1 mark)

2   April is designing a training programme for herself as part of her GCSE coursework.

    a)   What do the initials FITT stand for?

Frequency, Intensity, Time and Type.

(1 mark)

    b)   Explain why you would need to use knowledge of FITT when designing a training
programme.

To improve and get fitter you need to increase the frequency,

intensity and time that you train for in order to keep overloading.

You also need to vary the type of activity, so that you don't

over-stress the tissues and joints used in the main sport, and to

help prevent boredom.

Make sure you cover all four of the FITT principles in your answer.

(4 marks)

Exam Questions

1   Lisa has been unable to train for four weeks due to a groin strain.

    a)   What is likely to have happened to her fitness level?

....

(1 mark)

    b)   Explain why athletes need to balance the effects of reversibility with the need for rest and recovery.

....

....

(2 marks)

2   Janice is training for the London Marathon. Every other day she runs 10 miles, followed by a 15 minute walk to cool down. She is getting bored with the training and doesn't feel that she is improving.

    a)   How could Janice improve her training programme?

....

....

....

(2 marks)

    b)   State **one** benefit of a cool-down.

....

(1 mark)

3   A sprinter's training programme includes a lot of anaerobic activity to make it specific to his needs. Specificity is one of the five principles of training. Name and explain the other four principles of training which the sprinter should consider.

....

....

....

....

....

....

....

....

(8 marks)

Training Methods

Training should make you <u>better</u> at whatever it is you're training for. For this to happen, you need to match the type of training with what you want to do. There are <u>nine</u> training methods you need to know.

1) *Weight Training Improves Muscular Strength*

When you weight train, you <u>contract</u> your muscles.
There are two ways to do weight training — each type uses a different kind of muscle contraction.

1) You can train by <u>increasing the tension</u> in a muscle, <u>without</u> changing the muscle's <u>length</u> (so there's <u>no movement</u>). You can do this by pressing against stationary objects.

> <u>EXAMPLE</u>: The Wall Sit
> Sit with your back to the wall and your knees bent at 90° and hold it.

2) You can also train by contracting your muscles to make your limbs <u>move</u>.

> <u>EXAMPLE</u>: Pull-ups
> Hang from a bar and then pull yourself up until your head is over it.

3) Each completed movement is called a '<u>rep</u>' (repetition), and you've got to finish a '<u>set</u>' (group of reps) before a rest.

4) Both types of weight training can be used to develop <u>muscular strength</u> and <u>muscular endurance</u>.

5) For the training to improve your fitness, you need to <u>overload</u> (see p59).

6) Weight training is a type of <u>anaerobic training</u>. It's good for improving performance in anaerobic activities such as <u>sprinting</u>. It can also just be a great way to improve your <u>health-related fitness</u>.

<u>OVERLOAD</u> is achieved by lifting the weights <u>more times</u> (increasing the reps or sets), or using <u>heavier</u> weights.

2) *Continuous Training Means No Resting*

1) <u>Continuous training</u> involves exercising at a <u>constant rate</u> doing activities like <u>running</u> or <u>cycling</u>.

2) It usually means exercising so that your <u>heart rate</u> is between 60% and 80% of its maximum.

3) Of course, you need to <u>overload</u> during training to get fitter.

4) As well as improving your <u>cardiovascular fitness</u> and <u>muscular endurance</u>, it's also good for using up <u>body fat</u> and improving your <u>body composition</u>.

<u>OVERLOAD</u> is achieved by increasing the <u>duration</u>, distance, <u>speed</u>, or <u>frequency</u> of the training.

5) Continuous training is <u>only</u> made up of <u>aerobic activity</u> — so it's good training for activities like marathon running.

Learn this now — and take a weight off your mind...
There's lots more of these training methods coming up. For each method, make sure you learn how to do it, how to achieve overload and whether it's good training for <u>aerobic</u> or <u>anaerobic</u> activities.

Training Methods

3) Fartlek Training is all about Changes of Speed

1) <u>Fartlek training</u> can be made easy or hard to suit your fitness and can be adapted to fit any <u>continuous</u> exercise (e.g. running, cycling, swimming, rowing).

2) It involves changes in <u>intensity</u> and type of exercise <u>without stopping</u>.

> For example, part of a fartlek run could be to <u>sprint</u> for <u>10 seconds</u>, then <u>jog</u> for <u>20 seconds</u> (repeated for 4 minutes) — followed by <u>long-stride running</u> for <u>2 minutes</u>.

<u>OVERLOAD</u> is achieved by increasing the <u>times</u> or <u>speeds</u> of each bit, or the <u>terrain difficulty</u> (e.g. running uphill).

3) It's a <u>mix</u> of <u>aerobic</u> and <u>anaerobic</u> activity, so it's good training for activities that need <u>different paces</u>, like football and basketball.

4) The really good thing about fartlek training is that it can be <u>easily changed</u> to suit an <u>individual</u> or <u>activity</u>.

4) Circuit Training Uses Loads of Different Exercises

1) Each circuit has between 6 and 10 <u>stations</u> in it. At each station you do a <u>specific exercise</u> for a <u>set amount of time</u> before moving onto the next station. You're allowed a <u>short rest</u> between stations.

<u>OVERLOAD</u> is achieved by doing <u>more repetitions</u> at each station, completing the circuit <u>more quickly</u>, <u>resting less</u> between stations, or by repeating the circuit.

2) All the exercises are <u>different</u>, which makes circuit training a lot more <u>interesting</u> than some other training methods.

3) Circuit training can be <u>easily adapted</u> to suit you.

> A circuit's 'stations' might include <u>weight training</u>, or <u>aerobic</u> exercises...
> Because you <u>design</u> the circuit, you can use circuit training to improve <u>muscular endurance</u>, <u>strength</u>, <u>cardiovascular fitness</u>... anything you want really.

5) Cross Training Improves Overall Performance

1) <u>No single exercise</u> will improve <u>all</u> components of health-related and skill-related fitness <u>equally well</u>.

2) By picking activities that use different <u>muscle groups</u> or focus on different components of fitness, you can improve your <u>general overall fitness</u> — this is <u>cross training</u>.

3) In cross training, you can do activities that focus on one muscle group while waiting for another set of muscles to recover. This means you can <u>train more</u>, but without the risk of getting <u>injured</u>.

4) Because you're doing different activities, it can be a lot more <u>interesting</u> than some of the other training methods.

5) Whatever activities you do as part of cross training, you still need to <u>overload</u> to improve your fitness.

6) As with circuit training, you can <u>adapt</u> cross training to improve whichever skill or component of fitness you want to.

<u>EXAMPLE:</u> A swimmer might decide to take up <u>squash</u> and <u>cycling</u>. These activities still help improve <u>cardiovascular fitness</u> but use different muscles to swimming.

You can make circuit training really specific to you and your sport...
In case you're wondering, <u>fartlek</u> means '<u>speed play</u>' in Swedish.

Training Methods

6) *Plyometric Training* Improves *Power*

For lots of sports it's important to have <u>explosive strength</u> and <u>power</u> (see p32), e.g. for fast starts in sprinting. You can train muscular power using <u>plyometrics</u>.

1) When muscles contract, they can either <u>shorten</u> or <u>lengthen</u>, e.g. during a bicep curl.

- During the upward movement of a bicep curl the muscle <u>contracts</u> and gets <u>shorter</u>.
- During the downward movement the bicep muscle still <u>tenses</u> and <u>contracts</u> to control putting the dumbbell down. Instead of getting shorter, the muscle gets <u>stretched</u> and <u>lengthens</u> — this is an <u>eccentric</u> muscle contraction.

Bicep muscle

2) When a muscle gets stretched during an eccentric muscle contraction, extra <u>energy</u> is stored in the muscle (just like storing energy in an elastic band by stretching it).

3) This extra energy means the muscle can generate a <u>greater force</u> when it contracts normally.

4) The energy stored in an eccentric muscle contraction doesn't last forever — the <u>faster</u> the muscle can change between the two types of contractions, the more <u>powerful</u> the movement.

5) Plyometric training improves the <u>speed</u> you can change between the two types of contraction. It puts <u>a lot</u> of <u>stress</u> on the muscles and tendons though, so you need to do a really good <u>warm-up</u>.

6) Plyometrics is a type of <u>anaerobic training</u> and probably won't leave you out of breath. It <u>isn't</u> really needed for health-related fitness.

<u>EXAMPLE</u>: Squat Jumps
Your quadriceps eccentrically contract when you bend your knees, and normally contract when you jump. Squat jumps improve the power of your quads and increase how high you can jump.

7) *Interval Training* uses *Fixed Patterns* of *Exercise*

1) Fixed patterns of <u>high intensity</u> and <u>low intensity</u> exercise intervals are used in interval training.

2) For example, you might alternate <u>sprinting 200 m</u> with <u>jogging 100 m</u>, or in swimming, maybe alternate <u>sprinting</u> a set number of lengths with <u>resting</u> for a fixed length of time.

3) By doing <u>aerobic</u> exercise while recovering from <u>anaerobic</u> exercise, you push your heart and lungs more and improve your cardiovascular fitness loads — so it's good training for <u>team sports</u> like rugby.

<u>OVERLOAD</u> is achieved by increasing the <u>proportion of time</u> spent on the <u>high intensity</u> exercise, or by increasing the <u>intensity</u> (e.g. running faster).

4) But you need to <u>overload</u> to improve your fitness.

5) The downside is it's very <u>exhausting</u>.

Interval training — revision, questions, revision, questions...
Eccentric contractions can seem a bit odd, but stick with it and it'll click eventually.

Training Methods

8) Flexibility and Mobility Training Improves Suppleness

Flexibility and mobility training uses various stretches to improve your flexibility.
There are three different types of stretch you need to know about:

1) **STATIC**

A static stretch involves gradually stretching a muscle, and then holding
the stretch position for a few seconds before relaxing it.

- In an **ACTIVE** static stretch you use your own muscles to hold the stretch
  position. E.g. raising your leg in front of you to stretch your hamstring.

- In a **PASSIVE** static stretch, you use
  someone else or a piece of equipment
  to help you hold the stretch position.

Stretched muscle

Stretched muscle

2) **DYNAMIC**

Dynamic stretching means slowly increasing the range of a
movement that stretches the muscle.

E.g. swinging one leg forwards and
backwards, making it swing higher
each time.

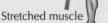
Stretched muscle

3) **PROPRIOCEPTIVE NEUROMUSCULAR FACILITATION (PNF)**

For this kind of stretching you need to contract the muscle before you stretch it.

E.g. get a partner to raise one of your legs until you feel a
stretch in your hamstring. Then contract your hamstring
for a few seconds — your partner should hold your leg
firm so it doesn't move. Relax your hamstring and get
your partner to lift your leg slightly higher to stretch the
muscle a little bit more.

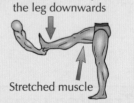
Muscle contraction pushes
the leg downwards

Stretched muscle

9) Altitude Training Increases Cardiovascular Endurance

1) At higher altitudes the air pressure is lower — which means you take in
   less oxygen with each breath.

2) The body makes more red blood cells so enough oxygen can still be
   supplied to the body.

3) Athletes train at high altitude to increase their red blood cell count, then
   compete at low altitude while they still have some of these extra red
   blood cells. This means they have a much better oxygen supply to their
   muscles, which increases their ability to do aerobic activity.

Altitude training lets you aim for the top...

Make sure you can remember the different types of stretching — static active, static passive,
dynamic and PNF. And learn why altitude training improves your cardiovascular endurance.

Training Methods

This is the last page on training methods...

*Training Helps Improve your **Mental Capacity***

1) Training can not only help you to improve <u>physically</u>, but <u>mentally</u> too.

2) For a lot of sports and physical activities, there comes a point where you 'hit a wall'.
You're <u>tired</u>, and <u>voices</u> inside your head start shouting at you to <u>stop</u> and <u>rest</u>.

3) By training, you can increase your ability to <u>keep going</u> even when you're tired.

4) You can also put <u>pressure</u> on yourself during training. This will help you be able to <u>cope with</u> competition pressure, which'll <u>improve</u> your <u>competence</u> and <u>performance</u>.

Training** Should be **Fun

As well as all those training methods there are loads of other fun <u>activities</u> and <u>classes</u> you can do to improve your fitness.

YOGA AND PILATES

Both yoga and pilates use a series of <u>exercises</u> and <u>stretches</u> that help increase <u>strength</u> and <u>flexibility</u>. Yoga exercises the whole body, while Pilates focuses more on the core torso muscles, e.g. abdominals.

AEROBICS/AQUA AEROBICS

This involves doing aerobic <u>exercises to music</u>. It's good for improving <u>strength</u>, <u>flexibility</u> and <u>cardiovascular endurance</u>. Aqua aerobics is just aerobics in a swimming pool — it puts <u>less strain</u> on your joints so it's good for avoiding injuries.

SPIN

This is a high intensity workout using exercise bikes which are set to different levels of resistance. It's good for improving both your <u>cardiovascular</u> and <u>anaerobic</u> fitness.

BODY PUMP

This is a <u>choreographed</u> workout that combines <u>weight training</u> and <u>aerobics</u>. It's good for improving <u>strength</u> and <u>cardiovascular endurance</u>.

DANCE EXERCISE

This is an aerobic workout that is based on <u>dance moves</u>. It's good for <u>cardiovascular endurance</u>.

Training can help your mind and body...

Training doesn't just have to be about being stuck in the gym lifting weights or going round and round on the running track. There are lots of classes and sports that still count as training and can be much more fun.

Training Plans

Now you've seen the different types of training, it's time to bring them together to make a PEP (see p59).

Training Plans Help Improve Specific Areas of Fitness

Example: John is 15 and wants to improve at football.

He wants a 12 week PEP and can train 3 times a week.

He's tested his fitness by doing some 30 m sprints to test speed and Sargent jumps to test power. He's also done a Coopers 12 minute run test and has decided that he needs to improve his cardiovascular fitness.

Here's a PEP John could use:

	Week One	Week Two	Week Three	Week Four
Session 1	Circuit training — focus on skills and sprinting	Circuit training — focus on skills and sprinting	Circuit training — focus on skills and sprinting	Rest
Session 2	Fartlek training	Fartlek training	Fartlek training	Rest
Session 3	Cross training — swimming	Spin class	Continuous training — running	Testing

When making a PEP try to remember:

Specificity — You need to match the plan to the person, the sport they want to play and what they want to improve.

Testing — so you can spot any areas you might want to work on, and monitor any improvement in your fitness.

Each training session will start with an appropriate warm-up and finish with a cool-down.

The four week plan is repeated three times — each week the intensity and difficulty is increased to cause overload and improve John's fitness.

Every four weeks he rests and re-tests himself so he can monitor any improvements and adjust the difficulty and plan if it's needed.

There are Three Stages of Training for Competition

Most sports don't compete all year round, so athletes change their training plans depending on whether it's before, during or after the competition season — this is called periodisation.

1) **Pre-season preparation** — Anaerobic, aerobic and skills training — plus some extra strength training.

2) **Competition/Peak Season** — Compete regularly, while maintaining fitness and getting enough rest. Training can be planned so that you 'peak' at the right time (e.g. for key competitions).

3) **Closed-season (out of season)** — Recover from the strain of competition through rest and relaxation. Do some aerobic and strength training to maintain fitness and get ready for the next pre-season training.

I love it when a plan comes together...

Writing a PEP can be a tricky thing. Try flicking back through the different training methods to see which ones train the things you want to improve, and don't forget to include some testing so you can see how you're getting better. Your training plan might also depend on when in the season you're making it for.

Training Zones and Recovery

As you exercise, your muscles need <u>more oxygen</u>, so your heart beats <u>faster</u> to get it to them. You only need to know the stuff on this page if you're doing the AQA or Edexcel courses.

Heart Rate — *Heartbeats per Minute*

1) Your <u>resting heart rate</u> is the <u>number of times your heart beats per minute</u> when at <u>rest</u> (i.e. when you're <u>not</u> doing any physical activity).

2) An adult's resting heart rate is normally between 60 and 80 beats per minute (bpm).

3) When you exercise, your <u>heart rate increases</u> to increase the <u>blood</u> and <u>oxygen supply</u> to your muscles.

4) The <u>more efficient</u> your cardiovascular system, the <u>slower</u> your pulse rate will be (either resting or exercising), and the <u>quicker</u> it will <u>return to normal</u> after you've been exercising.

5) You can find your theoretical <u>maximum heart rate</u> by subtracting your age from <u>220</u>.

6) The <u>difference</u> between your maximum heart rate and your resting heart rate is called your <u>working heart rate</u>.

> **Working Heart Rate** = Maximum − Resting

Training Zones — *get your Pulse in the Target Zone*

1) To <u>improve</u> your cardiovascular fitness and do <u>aerobic</u> training, you have to <u>work</u> your <u>heart and lungs</u> hard for <u>at least 15 minutes</u>.

2) To aerobically train, you need to make sure your heart rate is in the <u>target zone</u> (or the <u>aerobic training zone</u>).

> **TARGET ZONE** — between <u>60%</u> and <u>80%</u> of your <u>maximum heart rate</u>.

3) The <u>boundaries</u> between the training zones are called <u>training thresholds</u>. To overload (see page 59) and improve either your <u>aerobic</u> or <u>anaerobic fitness</u>, you have to cross the <u>lower threshold</u> of the relevant training zone.

4) If you're just <u>starting</u> a training programme, you should be training with your heart rate near to the <u>60%</u> training threshold. <u>Professional athletes</u> will train <u>above</u> the <u>80%</u> threshold in the <u>anaerobic</u> training zone to improve their bodies' ability to <u>deal</u> with <u>lactic acid</u> (see page 23).

Get in the zone...
It's important you know what training zones are and whether they train aerobic or anaerobic fitness.

Training Zones and Recovery

You're also going to need to know about <u>recovery</u>. But you only have to be able to draw graphs to show it if you're doing an AQA or Edexcel course.

Recovery Rate Depends on Fitness

1) It takes a while for your heart rate to return to <u>normal</u> when you stop exercising.

2) The length of <u>time</u> it takes for your heart rate to return to normal (your resting heart rate) is your <u>recovery rate</u>. The <u>fitter</u> you are, the <u>faster</u> your heart rate falls.

3) You can look at comparative fitness by using lovely <u>graphs</u> like these.

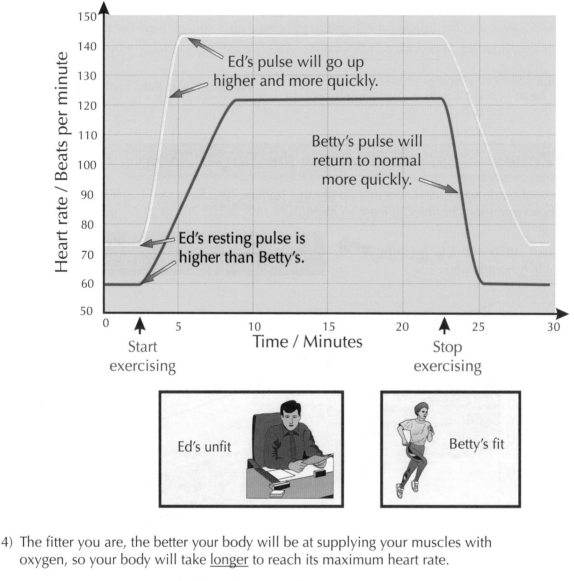

4) The fitter you are, the better your body will be at supplying your muscles with oxygen, so your body will take <u>longer</u> to reach its maximum heart rate.

5) Your recovery time not only depends on your fitness, but how <u>strenuous</u> the activity was too.

6) The more strenuous the activity, the more <u>anaerobic activity</u> your body will have been doing. You'll still need lots of oxygen when you <u>stop</u> exercising to get rid of the <u>lactic acid</u> build up.

It's surprising how long it can take to fully recover...

So the <u>fitter</u> you are, the <u>slower</u> your heart rate goes up and the <u>faster</u> it comes back down again. Lovely.

Warm-Up and Worked Exam Questions

Warm-Up Questions

1) Describe the difference between a 'rep' and a 'set' in weight training.
2) Give one advantage of cross training.
3) Describe an eccentric muscle contraction.
4) Name three types of flexibility and mobility training.
5) Name two anaerobic training methods.
6) What aspects of fitness can aqua aerobics be used to improve?
7) Name the three stages of training for competitive athletes.
8) What does the term 'working heart rate' mean?

Worked Exam Questions

Here's another lot of questions for you to have a go at, with a few worked examples to start you off...

1 Sharon wants to improve her cardiovascular endurance using fartlek training, but she has been told that it can be difficult to see how hard you are training using this method.

a) Name **two** other types of training that would improve her cardiovascular endurance.

Circuit training or continuous training.

*You could also put interval training,
cross training or altitude training here.* (2 marks)

b) Give **two** advantages of fartlek training.

*It's good training for sports that need different speeds and it can
be easily changed to suit the individual.*

Make sure you know the advantages and the disadvantages for all types of training. (2 marks)

2 When training to improve cardiovascular endurance, you should train in your aerobic training zone. Explain how to calculate the thresholds of this training zone.

First calculate your maximum heart rate. This is 220 – your age.

The lower threshold of the aerobic training zone is 60% of your maximum

heart rate. The upper threshold is 80% of your maximum heart rate

(3 marks)

3 Exercise causes changes to the body.
Give **two** factors that affect recovery time after exercise.

Intensity of exercise.

The person's fitness

(2 marks)

Exam Questions

1   Which of the following training methods is **most** suitable for increasing aerobic fitness?

    A   Plyometric training

    B   Weight training

    C   Continuous training

    D   Circuit training

(1 mark)

2   Which of the following training methods is **most** suitable for improving power?

    A   Plyometric training

    B   Altitude training

    C   Fartlek training

    D   Continuous training

(1 mark)

3   Suggest **one** method of training that could be used to improve strength.
State whether this is an aerobic or anaerobic training method.

....

....

(2 marks)

4   George is training for the school cross-country team.

    a)   Which type of endurance training would be the most suitable for this, and why?

....

....

(2 marks)

    b)   Give **one** disadvantage of this type of training.

....

(1 mark)

    c)   After a few weeks, George realises that he is no longer achieving overload,
so he decides to train three times a week, instead of two.
Describe **one** other way that George could alter his training to achieve overload.

....

....

(1 mark)

Exam Questions

5   Fiona is a hockey player. Her friend Vicky runs cross-country. They want to train together to encourage each other.

 a)   Suggest a type of endurance training that would suit both sports.

 ....

 (1 mark)

 b)   The girls decide to do a continuous training session once a week.
  Suggest **one** aspect of Fiona's performance that this type of training will **not** develop.

 ....

 (1 mark)

6   The diagram below shows the heart rates of two students, before, during and after completing an identical training session.

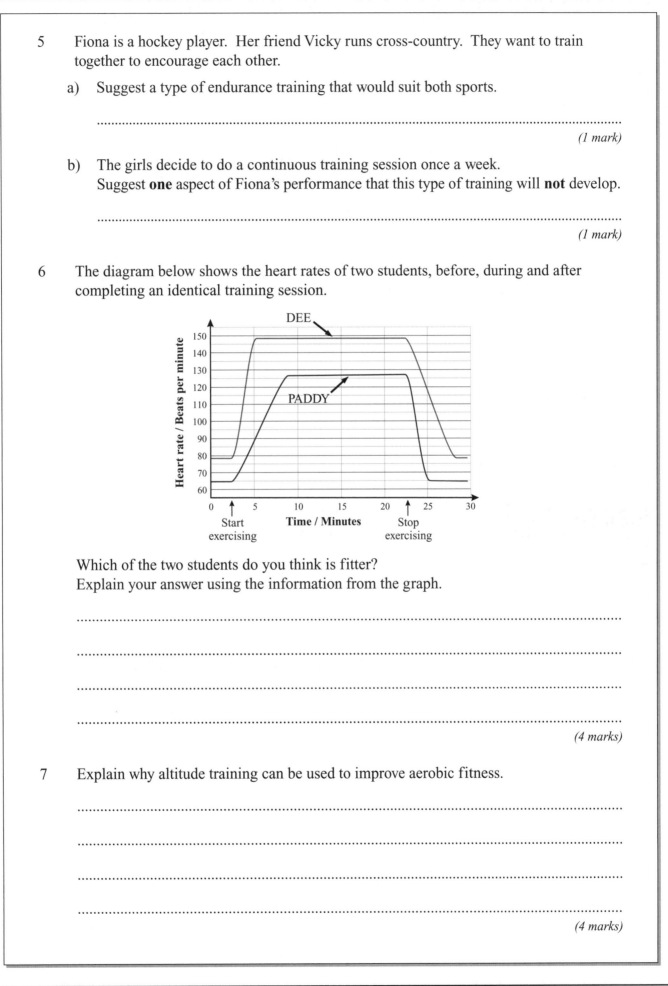

 Which of the two students do you think is fitter?
 Explain your answer using the information from the graph.

 ....

 ....

 ....

 ....

 (4 marks)

7   Explain why altitude training can be used to improve aerobic fitness.

 ....

 ....

 ....

 ....

 (4 marks)

Types of Skill

Skills are all the things you use when you do an activity or play a sport — some are <u>simple</u>, like running, but others are more <u>complicated</u>, like serving in tennis and somersaults in gymnastics. If you're doing an Edexcel or AQA course you can miss this page out.

A **Skill** is Something You **Learn**

You need to know this definition of <u>skill</u>:

> A **SKILL** is a <u>learned</u> ability to bring about the <u>result</u> you want, with maximum <u>certainty</u> and <u>efficiency</u>.

So the main point is that a skill is something you've <u>got to learn</u>.
You can't be born with a skill, although you might learn it faster than other people.

There are <u>five</u> characteristics that make a movement skilful:

1) **PRE-DETERMINED** — With any skilled movement, you always have a <u>pre-determined result in mind</u> — you know what you want to do <u>before</u> you start. E.g. if you're passing the ball to someone in hockey you know what type of pass you're going to use and who you want to pass it to.

2) **EFFICIENT** — A skilled movement should be <u>efficient</u> and use the <u>minimum</u> amount of <u>energy/time</u>. E.g. a good swimming technique can help you swim faster and for longer.

3) **COORDINATED** — Skilled movements are <u>coordinated</u> — they use <u>two or more</u> parts of the body together to get the <u>maximum effect</u>. E.g. a vault in gymnastics requires good arm and leg coordination to produce the lift needed to get the technique right.

4) **FLUENT** — A skilled athlete is able to <u>flow</u> from one skilled movement to another, e.g. punch combinations in boxing.

5) **AESTHETIC** — On top of all this, skilled movements <u>look good</u>. In some sports, like gymnastics and figure skating, your skill is <u>judged</u> by the appearance of your movements. <u>Skilled</u> players make skilled movements and techniques <u>look easy</u>, while <u>less skilled</u> players and performers can look <u>awkward</u> and <u>uncomfortable</u>.

Fundamental Motor Skills — Basic Skills like Running

1) You tend to master a lot of <u>fundamental motor skills</u> at an <u>early age</u> when you learn to move about.

2) Fundamental motor skills tend to be <u>transferable</u> between many different activities. Just think of all the sports where you need basic skills like:

| **Running** | **Jumping** | **Throwing** | **Catching** | **Kicking** | **Hitting** |

3) You can <u>analyse</u> how good you are at some of these skills by doing simple tests. E.g. <u>timing how long</u> it takes you to run a set distance, or <u>measuring how far</u> you can <u>jump</u> or <u>throw a ball</u>.

4) When learning a <u>new sport</u> or <u>activity</u>, it's really <u>important</u> that you've mastered all the basic skills needed, <u>before</u> you attempt more complex ones.

Some skills can take a long time to learn...

So any skilled movement should have a <u>pre-determined</u> goal, be <u>efficient</u>, <u>coordinated</u>, <u>fluent</u> and <u>look good</u>. Make sure you can remember the <u>fundamental motor skills</u> listed on this page.

Types of Skill

Things like your <u>environment</u> or your <u>opponents</u> can have an affect on how you perform a <u>skill</u>.
If you're doing an Edexcel course you don't need to know about skills for the exam, so skip on to p80...

Skills are **Open**, **Closed** or Somewhere **In Between**

1) An <u>open skill</u> is one which is affected by <u>many external factors</u>.
   E.g. in golf, you can't just go up to the ball and take a swing, oblivious
   to what's going on around you. You need to consider things like the
   position of the hole, obstacles like trees, and the effect of the wind.

Most gymnastic events like the beam involve many different closed skills.

2) A <u>closed skill</u> is one <u>hardly affected</u> by the <u>environment</u> or <u>external factors</u>. E.g. in squash, you usually make the <u>same movements</u> — you don't need to change them for different conditions.

3) To confuse the issue, <u>most skills</u> actually fall somewhere <u>in between</u>. E.g. taking a football penalty — your environment <u>doesn't</u> change much, but you can <u>alter</u> your movement to change the speed and aim of the shot. So it's <u>partly closed</u> and <u>partly open</u>.

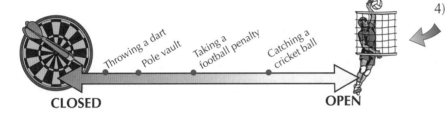

4) You can compare the "openness" of skills by putting them on a continuous <u>scale</u>.

You Need to **Decide What** Skills to Use and **When**

In sports you have to make lots of <u>decisions</u> all the time. Whether you're a <u>performer</u>, <u>leader/coach</u> or an <u>official</u> — there's always something you have to make your mind up about.

<u>**PERFORMERS**</u> — make decisions about their <u>individual performance</u>.

1) You have to think about <u>tactics</u> and <u>strategies</u> '<u>on the go</u>'. E.g. who to pass to next or when to 'close down' the opposition in <u>invasion games</u> — games where you enter your opponents half of the pitch like football or hockey. In <u>target games</u> (games where you aim to hit or throw something), e.g. golf, you decide what shot to play based the weather conditions and where the ball is. You also need to <u>respond</u> to what others are doing, e.g. reading a opponents tennis serve.

2) You also have to make decisions <u>before you start</u>, e.g. in activities like ice skating or gymnastics, you need to decide what to put in your routine when you're <u>composing</u> it. You also need to be <u>creative</u> when you're planning it so that it stands out from the other competitors.

<u>**COACH/LEADERS**</u> — make decisions that will affect the <u>whole team</u>.

1) You can <u>plan</u> different <u>tactics</u> and <u>strategies</u> to improve the performance of your team, e.g. choosing a formation, or making someone mark an important player on the opposing team so they can't have a big impact on the game.

2) You can also make decisions <u>during the game</u>, e.g. using a time-outs strategically in basketball to try and disrupt the flow of the game or choosing to substitute a player into a match.

<u>**OFFICIALS**</u> — have to make lots of decisions <u>during</u> a game.

They're responsible for making sure the <u>rules are followed</u>, and need to decide if they have been broken, e.g. deciding if a player is offside in football, or when there's a foul in netball.

Learning Skills and Feedback

Learning a new skill isn't easy. It takes <u>practice</u>, <u>practice</u>, <u>practice</u>... or <u>copying</u>... or <u>trial and error</u>...
If you're doing the Edexcel or WJEC courses, you don't need to know the stuff on this page.

There are *Different Ways* to *Learn* a *Skill*

1) Practice/Rehearsal

Practising means <u>repeating</u> a skill until you can do it. Try to make sure you've got a <u>trainer</u> or
coach to help show you the correct technique to use. They'll also be able to make sure you're
practising the <u>right skills</u> for your sport and sort out any problems in your technique.

There are <u>four</u> different types of practice you need to know about:

WHOLE

This means practising the whole technique in <u>one go</u>. It's good
because you practise <u>all</u> the different parts of a skill at the <u>same</u>
<u>time</u> — so you can get a <u>feel</u> for what the whole skill is like.
Some skills are best learnt as a whole, e.g. kicking a ball.

PART

If you're learning a <u>complex</u> skill it can help to <u>break</u> the whole skill down into
<u>parts</u> and practise each bit <u>separately</u>, e.g. the ball toss and racket motion of a
tennis serve. You can put all the individual bits together once you've got each
one — so it's still important to know what the whole skill looks like.

VARIABLE

This involves repeating the technique in all of the
<u>different situations</u> that you might need to use it in.

FIXED

This means repeating the same technique in <u>one situation</u>
over and over again — it's sometimes known as a <u>drill</u>.

2) Copying Others

Another way to learn a new skill is to <u>watch others</u> doing it and then try to <u>repeat it</u>.

1) It's a <u>good</u> way to learn a skill if you're <u>starting</u> a new sport because it
   shows you what the correct technique <u>looks like</u> and what to aim for.
2) Even if you've got a grip of the basics, you can improve by watching
   <u>top athletes</u> or skilled <u>role models</u>, and trying to copy their techniques,
   e.g. copying different types of bowling action in cricket.

3) Trial and Error

This is when you repeat a technique, but <u>change it slightly</u> each time to find out what works and
what doesn't. It can be quite a <u>long process</u>, but it's a good way to improve and develop a skill,
e.g. shooting an arrow or taking free kicks.

Learn this page by practising writing it out...

There are four different ways you can <u>practise</u> a skill — whole, part, variable and fixed. But if you are
trying to learn a new skill, you'll probably use a mixture of all of them. Make sure you also know
about the other two ways of learning a skill — <u>copying</u> and <u>trial and error</u>.

Learning Skills and Feedback

To get better at a skill, you need to get <u>feedback</u> so you know what you're doing right and what you need to improve on. If you're doing an Edexcel course you can just jump ahead to page 80.

There are Different Ways to **Develop** a Skill

Once you've got the basics, you can <u>improve</u> and <u>develop</u> a skill or technique by increasing one or more of these things:

1) **<u>RANGE</u>** — e.g. once you know how to fire a bow in archery, you can try moving the target further away.

2) **<u>DIFFICULTY</u>** — e.g. adding a twist to a dive.

3) **<u>CONSISTENCY</u>** — this means being able to <u>reliably</u> do a technique, e.g. getting serves 'in' in badminton.

4) **<u>PRECISION</u>** — this means being more <u>accurate</u>, e.g. improving your aim in target games.

5) **<u>CONTROL</u>** — improving control will let you move on to more <u>advanced</u> versions of that skill, e.g. going from controlling a football at jogging speed, to running speed.

6) **<u>FLUENCY</u>** — this means being able to perform a skill <u>smoothly</u> and <u>flow</u> from one technique to the next without having to stop and think in between, e.g. combinations in boxing.

> **<u>QUALITY</u>** — By developing <u>all</u> the other aspects of a skill you will improve the <u>overall quality</u> of the skill too.

Feedback — Finding Out How You Did

Feedback can be either <u>intrinsic</u> or <u>extrinsic</u>:

> **<u>INTRINSIC</u>** — <u>you</u> know how well you did the technique because of what it '<u>felt</u>' like.
> **<u>EXTRINSIC</u>** — <u>someone else</u> tells you or shows you what happened, and how to <u>improve</u>.

There are <u>two</u> parts of a skill or movement that feedback can focus on:

1 **<u>KNOWLEDGE OF PERFORMANCE</u>** — did you use the correct technique?

<u>Intrinsic feedback</u> — e.g. <u>you</u> know you didn't kick the ball with the right part of your foot.

<u>Extrinsic feedback</u> — e.g. a <u>coach</u> or <u>trainer</u> telling you which bits of the movement you did well, and which bits weren't so good.

2 **<u>KNOWLEDGE OF RESULTS</u>** — what was the outcome?

This is usually <u>extrinsic</u>. It can come from <u>coaches</u> and <u>trainers</u>, e.g. a 400 m runner being told their time, or javelin thrower getting their distance.

You can use all this feedback to work out your <u>strengths</u> and <u>weaknesses</u> and come up with an <u>action plan</u> to improve your performance.

There are quite a few terms here to get your head around...

<u>Intrinsic</u> means from you, <u>extrinsic</u> means from something external. <u>Knowledge of performance</u> is knowing how well you did something, <u>knowledge of results</u> is knowing what the outcome was.

Warm-Up and Worked Exam Questions

1) Name five characteristics that make a movement skilful.
2) Which type of skill is affected by the environment — open or closed?
3) Give one decision that will need to be made by a referee during a cricket match.
4) Give an example of a part practice exercise.
5) Name the six different ways that you can improve and develop a skill once you've learnt the basics of it.
6) What is intrinsic feedback?

Worked Exam Questions

It's time to test what's covered on the last five pages. You know the drill, worked examples first, then you're on your own.

1 Skills can be classified as either open or closed.
Explain the difference between an open and a closed skill.
Give **one** example of each type of skill from physical activities.

An open skill is something that is affected by external factors,

e.g. catching a ball could be affected by the wind. A closed skill is

hardly affected by external factors, e.g. a forward roll.

Don't forget to include those examples — they're worth half the marks.   *(4 marks)*

2 Describe **two** decisions that a player may have to make during a tennis match.

Where to aim their shot, reading their opponents serve and

deciding how to respond to it.

(2 marks)

3 Describe the characteristics of a skilful movement.

A skilful movement should be efficient and take the minimum amount

of energy and time to perform. It should be pre-determined — there

should always be a result in mind before the movement is started.

All parts of the body used in the movement should be coordinated to

produce a skilful movement that is fluent and looks good.

The question's worth five marks, so make sure you mention
all five characteristics.   *(5 marks)*

Exam Questions

1   Which of the following is a fundamental motor skill often used in gymnastics?

   A   Dancing

   B   Jumping

   C   Somersaulting

   D   Vaulting

   (1 mark)

2   Which of the following is **not** a form of extrinsic feedback from throwing a netball?

   A   Knowing a technique felt right.

   B   Scoring a goal.

   C   Your teacher analysing the throw.

   D   The netball going out of bounds when thrown.

   (1 mark)

3   Football players need many skills to be able to play and perform well.

   a)   Explain what is meant by the term "skill"?

   ....

   ....

   (2 marks)

   b)   Discuss whether taking a football penalty is a closed skill or an open skill.

   ....

   ....

   ....

   (3 marks)

4   A tennis coach uses different types of practice when teaching his players a new skill.
   Describe the **four** types of practice that the coach might use.

   ....

   ....

   ....

   ....

   (4 marks)

Feedback, Guidance and Motivation

You can be given feedback about your performance either <u>verbally</u>, <u>visually</u> or <u>manually</u>.
And the feedback you receive can provide encouragement and help <u>motivate</u> you.

Feedback can be *Visual*, *Verbal* or *Manual*

There are lots of different types of <u>feedback</u> and <u>guidance</u> a coach or trainer can
give when you're learning or developing a skill.

1) **VERBAL** — This is the type of feedback you're most likely to get. Usually someone will <u>watch you</u>
   and then <u>tell you</u> what you did right and wrong and how to improve your performance. If you're
   giving feedback to someone, you need to think about <u>what</u> you're saying and <u>how</u> you're saying it.

   - Use a suitable <u>volume</u> — some people won't respond to being shouted at,
     especially if you're stood right next to them.

   - Make sure what you say is <u>clear</u> — use <u>appropriate language</u> and <u>terminology</u>
     for who you're talking to so they can <u>understand</u> what you're saying.

   - <u>Project</u> your voice if you're talking to a group of people, so they can <u>all hear you</u>.

   - Make sure your <u>intonation</u> (the tone of your voice) is right so you don't
     come across as rude or unhelpful.

   - Try to talk about some good things as well as the bad so
     the feedback is <u>helpful</u> and <u>motivational</u>.

2) **VISUAL** — You can get lots of <u>visual clues</u> to help you perform a technique.
   E.g. a coach could use demonstrations or videos of your performance
   to show where you could improve your technique.

   You can also give and receive visual feedback during an activity,
   e.g. <u>signalling</u> where fielders should stand in cricket or making
   a <u>gesture</u> to encourage players to attack more in football.

3) **MANUAL** — This is when the trainer or coach <u>physically moves</u> your body <u>through</u>
   the <u>technique</u>, e.g. guiding your arms when you're practising a golf swing.

Feedback can Help *Motivate* You

1) <u>Motivation</u>'s about how <u>keen</u> you are to do something.
   It's what <u>drives you on</u> when things get difficult — your <u>desire</u> to succeed.

2) Just like feedback, motivation can be either <u>intrinsic</u> (from inside you) or <u>extrinsic</u> (from outside).

   > **INTRINSIC**
   > You want to get involved as an <u>official</u>, <u>player</u> or <u>leader</u> because it's something you
   > <u>enjoy</u> and you want to help — even if there are <u>no</u> prizes or rewards for taking part.

   > **EXTRINSIC**
   > Maybe you want to do well as a player or leader because there's a <u>big reward</u>, e.g. <u>prize</u>
   > <u>money</u> or <u>publicity</u>. Or maybe you're getting <u>paid</u> to referee a game so it can take place.

3) Good feedback can be a really good motivator — it can <u>spur you on</u> to
   work hard and really <u>focus</u> on the areas you want to improve.

Keep going — you're doing really well...
Make sure you can remember the <u>three different ways</u> of giving <u>feedback</u> — learn at least one example
for each of them. You need to know the difference between <u>intrinsic</u> and <u>extrinsic</u> motivation too.

Goal Setting

When the going gets tough — the tough get feedback and set <u>SMART</u> goals to help <u>motivate</u> themselves. If you're doing an AQA course you don't need to worry about this page.

Goal Setting Gives You a Target to Reach

1) <u>Goal setting</u> means setting <u>targets</u> that you want to reach. They can be <u>outcome goals</u>, like winning the game, or <u>performance goals</u> like beating a personal best.

2) Goal setting can be a great <u>motivator</u> — it gives you something to <u>aim for</u> and helps ensure <u>exercise adherence</u> (a fancy way of saying it makes you <u>stick</u> to your training programme).

3) <u>Short-term</u> goals that you can reach quite quickly are <u>steps</u> on the way to a <u>long-term</u> one. It's important to have short-term goals so you <u>don't</u> get <u>anxious</u> or <u>overwhelmed</u> by a long-term goal, like trying to win an Olympic medal.

4) And if all that wasn't enough, reaching a goal can boost your <u>confidence</u> and can give you a <u>sense of achievement</u>.

Use SMART to Set Your Goals

When you're setting targets — make sure they're <u>SMART</u>.

S **SPECIFIC**: Say <u>exactly</u> what you want to achieve.
1) Saying 'My goal is to be dead good at swimming' isn't very <u>useful</u>. It could mean <u>anything</u> — being able to swim very fast, for long distances, without stopping...
2) You need to be <u>specific</u> and outline <u>exactly</u> what you need to do to reach your target. E.g. 'My goal is to swim 1000 m without stopping'.

M **MEASURABLE**: Goals need to be <u>measurable</u> so you can know <u>when</u> you've achieved them.
E.g. Good target — 'My goal is to run 100 m in under 12 seconds'.
Bad target — 'My goal is to run the 100 m faster than I do now'.

A **ACHIEVABLE**: You need to make sure your targets set at the right level of <u>difficulty</u> — <u>too easy</u> and it won't <u>motivate</u> you, <u>too hard</u> and you might <u>give up</u>.

'A' can also stand for 'agreed' — you should agree your goals with your coach.

R **REALISTIC**: Set targets you can <u>realistically</u> reach.
1) This means you have everything you need to fulfil your target.
2) That could mean being <u>physically able</u> to so something.
3) It could be that you have enough <u>resources</u> (<u>time</u>, <u>money</u>, <u>facilities</u>...) to be able to reach your target.

'R' can also stand for 'recorded' — you should keep track of your progress.

T **TIME-BOUND**: Gives you a <u>deadline</u> for reaching your goal.
1) You need a time limit to make sure your target is <u>measurable</u>.
2) By meeting <u>short-term</u> target deadlines, you make sure you reach your <u>long-term goals</u> in time.

Having goals is a SMART thing...
This <u>SMART</u> approach to goal setting isn't just used in PE — it crops up everywhere, so it's worthwhile knowing about it. Make sure you know what the advantages of goal setting are and what the letters in SMART stand for. And don't forget to <u>use it</u> when you're setting targets for yourself.

Fatigue and Stress

It's easy to get stressed in a sports competition, which can have a negative effect on your performance. If you're doing the Edexcel or WJEC courses you don't have to know the stuff on this page for the exam.

Your Arousal Level Shouldn't be Too High

To perform well you need to have the right arousal level. Arousal is about being excited, keen and mentally ready (or unready) to perform a difficult task.

> 1) If your arousal level is low, then you're not very excited and you're unlikely to perform well.
>
> 2) If you're anxious and nervous your arousal level is too high. You might become tense and 'stressed out' which can cause you to 'choke' and be unable to perform skills you'd normally be able to, e.g. taking a penalty.
>
> 3) At the right arousal level you'll be determined and ready and should be able to perform your skills well.

Stress and Fatigue Affect Your Skill Levels

Being stressed or tired means you're either over or under aroused, which can really affect your skill levels. There are lots of factors that affect your skill level, here are the ones you need to know about.

1) **PERSONALITY** — You can describe people's personalities by saying how extroverted (outgoing) or introverted (shy) they are — most people are somewhere in between.

> - Extroverts often choose high excitement, fast paced team sports, e.g. rugby.
> - Introverts tend to get more nervous and stressed. They usually choose individual sports that rely on skill, precision and concentration, e.g. archery.

2) **EMOTIONS** — When you get stressed and tired you get more emotional. Getting too emotional can make you tense and anxious or aggressive — making it harder to concentrate and perform the skills you need to use.

3) **AGGRESSION** — Aggression can either be indirect (e.g. hitting a tennis ball) or direct (where there's actual physical contact between two players). In some athletes, like swimmers, aggression can just be a fierce determination to win. Aggression can have good and bad effects. It's good if it's kept under control because it can help to motivate you. But as you get stressed or tired, it can become harder to control — which is bad if it means you break the rules or injure an opponent.

4) **BOREDOM** — You get bored when you're mentally tired. If you're doing a repetitive activity, e.g. practising a golf swing, it can quickly become boring and tedious. Your concentration level drops and you stop performing the skill well.

5) **FEEDBACK** — Good feedback can help stop you getting stressed give you tips on how to improve your performance and help motivate you. Bad feedback and criticism can get you more stressed, harm your confidence and make your performance worse.

Mental Preparation can Stop You Getting Stressed

Mental preparation is all about getting in the 'zone'. It can help you keep control of your emotions and cope with stress so you can perform at your best.

> 1) Many athletes follow set routines to relax them or get them 'pumped up' for a performance.
>
> 2) Focusing on your strengths and imagining yourself performing well can help focus you on what you need to do and raise your confidence.

Preventing Injuries

There's a <u>risk</u> of injury whatever you do, so you need to know how to make exercising as <u>safe</u> as possible.

Do a **Risk Assessment** Before You Start

1) Whenever you do an activity there's always a <u>risk</u> of getting injured — it could be from <u>what</u> you're doing, <u>where</u> you're doing it or <u>who</u> you're doing it with.

2) Normally the more <u>challenging</u> an activity is, the <u>higher</u> the risks involved in doing the activity.

3) You need to do a <u>risk assessment</u>, then do things to <u>minimise</u> the risks so the activity is <u>as safe to do as possible</u> for both <u>yourself</u> and <u>others</u>.

A Lot of Injuries can be **Prevented**

There are lots of things you can do <u>before</u>, <u>during</u> and <u>after</u> exercise to lessen your chances of getting hurt.

Before the Activity:

1) Before doing a new activity, you should assess your personal readiness by filling in a <u>PAR-Q</u> (see p52).

2) <u>Warm-up</u> before the activity, making sure you <u>exercise the muscles</u> you're going to use.

3) Use the right <u>equipment</u> — and check it's not damaged and is in <u>good condition</u>.

4) Use the correct <u>technique</u> when <u>lifting</u>, <u>carrying</u> or <u>placing</u> equipment.
The techniques help stop you putting your back out or pulling a muscle.

5) Check for <u>possible dangers</u> in the area you're going to be exercising in.
   - <u>Officials</u> should check competition areas and equipment.
   - <u>Leaders</u> should check training and competition areas.
   - <u>Participants</u> should check their own equipment.

> E.g. you might need to check for dangers in:
> Gymnasiums/sports halls/fitness centres
> Playing fields
> Artificial outdoor areas
> Court areas
> Outdoor adventurous areas, e.g. mountain bike trails.

During the Activity:

1) Play with people of the same:
   - <u>Size</u> and <u>strength</u> — e.g. make sure you're in the right <u>weight division</u>, rather than against someone who's twice your size.
   - <u>Skill level</u> — don't try to play rugby against professionals on your first go.
   - <u>Gender</u> — generally men are physically stronger and faster than women, so many sports often have separate women's and men's divisions.

2) Sports <u>governing bodies</u> usually set down <u>rules</u> and <u>safety precautions</u> to <u>minimise</u> risks to players of their sport. You should follow these rules, be sporting and try not to hurt an opponent.

3) <u>Officials</u> (e.g. referees) can ensure there's <u>fair play</u> and the rules and safety precautions are followed e.g. giving yellow or red cards for bad tackles in football.

4) Use the correct <u>technique</u> — e.g. safely tackling someone in rugby or hockey.

5) Make sure you're not wearing anything that could get <u>caught</u> (e.g. jewellery, watches).

6) Wear suitable <u>footwear</u> — e.g. wearing studded football boots or spiked running shoes makes you less likely to slip and injure yourself.

7) Use <u>protective clothing/equipment</u> where appropriate, e.g. cycling helmets, mouth guards.

After the Activity:

1) <u>Cool-down</u> properly.

2) Keep a good level of <u>personal hygiene</u> by washing afterwards to help stop minor infections.

3) Give yourself plenty of <u>time to recover</u> before playing again.

Warm-Up and Worked Exam Questions

Warm-Up Questions

1) Who is more likely to play rugby — an extrovert or an introvert?
2) Explain how mental preparation can affect performance.
3) Name one extrinsic motivation for a player in a physical activity.
4) What does SMART stand for?
5) Why is it important for a target to be measurable?
6) Describe how feedback can motivate you.
7) Why it is important to wear the correct clothing when doing a physical activity?

Worked Exam Questions

Go through these worked exam questions carefully, and make sure that you understand the answers. Then try the exam questions on the next page.

1   Give **four** safety precautions that a participant could take to reduce their own risk of injury when taking part in a sport.

Participants should know and follow the rules of the game they are playing. They should wear appropriate protective clothing. A player should only play against people of a similar same skill level, size and strength to themselves. They player should remove any jewellery that they are wearing before the game begins.

There are lots of possible answers — make sure you put down at least four precautions to get all four marks.

(4 marks)

2   A coach can help to improve a player's performance by giving them verbal feedback.

a)   What is verbal feedback?

Telling someone how they could improve their performance.

(1 mark)

b)   Describe **two** other ways that feedback can be communicated to a player.

Feedback can be given visually, by signalling or demonstrating to a player how to improve performance. It can also be given manually, by physically moving someone's body through a technique.

(2 marks)

Exam Questions

1   Which of the following is **not** a characteristic of a SMART training goal?

     A   Measurable

     B   Achievable

     C   Reliable

     D   Time-bound

(1 mark)

2   What is the difference between intrinsic and extrinsic motivation?
Give an example of how each type could motivate a coach.

....

....

....

....

(4 marks)

3   Many performers feel nervous before taking part in sports competitions.

     a)   Explain how anxiety can affect a performer's skill level.

....

....

....

(2 marks)

     b)   Coaches often give motivational speeches to performers just before they compete.
Explain how motivation can affect a performer's skill level.

....

....

....

(2 marks)

4   Describe how goal-setting can help athletes to train and perform at their best.

....

....

....

....

(4 marks)

Injuries — Types and Treatment

You need to know the different types of injury, and if they affect the hard tissues (bones) or the soft tissues (everything else). If you're doing a WJEC course, you can jump straight to the revision summary.

Know What to Do if Someone Gets Injured

Doing any kind of physical activity means you <u>might</u> get injured.
But there are some things you can do beforehand in case someone gets hurt:

1) Try and have a <u>first aider</u> present — sports competitions and events often hire members of the St John Ambulance in case of any injuries.

2) Make sure you have a well stocked <u>first aid kit</u>. Keep it nearby, so you can get it quickly and easily.

3) Make sure you have access to a <u>phone</u> — if someone is seems seriously injured call 999 for an ambulance.

Most Sporting Injuries are to Soft Tissue

Your <u>soft tissues</u> are all the bits of you that <u>aren't bone</u> — muscles, skin, ligaments, tendons and stuff...
The most common injuries you can get are <u>cuts</u>, <u>bruises</u> and <u>swelling</u>.

1) <u>Cuts</u>, <u>grazes</u>, <u>blisters</u> and <u>chafing</u> can break the skin and cause bleeding.
Little ones will heal on their own but <u>large or deep cuts</u> will need <u>medical attention</u>.

2) <u>Bruising</u> is where your blood vessels get damaged — you bleed inside.

3) <u>Inflammation</u> is where the area around an injury <u>swells up</u> and is usually very sore.

Inactivity or Overuse can Injure Muscles and Tendons

1) If you never use your muscles, they'll eventually waste away, getting <u>smaller</u> and <u>weaker</u>. This is known as <u>muscle atrophy</u>.

2) And if you're not using your muscles, you won't be using your <u>tendons</u> either, so they'll get weaker too.

3) If your muscles and tendons are in this state, you're far more likely to <u>injure</u> or <u>strain</u> them, e.g. during strenuous activity, or by trying to lift heavy loads.

STRAIN

<u>Strained</u> (pulled) muscles and tendons are <u>tears</u> in the tissue — they're caused by sudden <u>overstretching</u>.

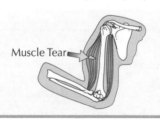
Muscle Tear

Pulled <u>hamstrings</u> and <u>calf muscles</u> are common injuries in loads of sports like football and cricket.

4) Whenever you <u>exercise</u>, you <u>damage</u> your muscles and tendons a little bit — it's what makes them <u>sore</u> the next day.

5) If you do <u>anaerobic exercise</u>, e.g. lifting weights, your muscles build up <u>lactic acid</u>. This eventually causes them to become <u>tired</u> and <u>stop contracting properly</u>. This is when you're most likely to <u>strain</u> and <u>injure</u> them.

6) Eventually this lactic acid build-up can cause your muscles to <u>stop working</u>, forcing you to stop exercising and <u>recover</u>. By regularly exercising anaerobically you can <u>increase</u> the amount of lactic acid your muscles can stand before this happens. Your body will also get better at <u>getting rid</u> of the lactic acid, which means you should be able to anaerobically exercise for <u>longer</u>.

Injuries — Types and Treatment

Here's some more stuff on <u>soft tissues</u> and also how to <u>treat</u> them using RICE... learn it well.
(Unless you're doing one of the WJEC courses of course, then you can skip these pages.)

Joint Injuries can be Caused by Overuse...

<u>Continuous stress</u> on part of the body over a <u>long</u> period of time can cause all sorts of problems:

1) If you injure or overuse your tendons they can become <u>inflamed</u> and sore — this is called <u>tendonitis</u>. Tennis players can develop <u>tennis elbow</u> — a painful inflammation of tendons in the elbow. Golfers get a similar injury called, wait for it... <u>golfer's elbow</u>.

2) Long-distance runners can develop a nasty bone injury in the leg called <u>shin splints</u>.

3) You're more at risk of these types of injury if you <u>train too hard</u> or <u>don't rest</u> enough between training sessions.

You can also develop bone diseases that affect your joints, like osteoarthritis.

... or Sudden Stress

1) <u>Sprains</u> are <u>joint</u> injuries where the <u>ligament</u> has been stretched or torn, usually because of violent twisting.

2) Joints can get <u>dislocated</u> as well. The bone is pulled out of its normal position — again, it's twisting that usually does it.

3) <u>Cartilage</u> can also be damaged. E.g. the cartilage of the <u>knee</u> can be <u>torn</u> by a violent <u>impact</u> or <u>twisting</u> motion.

This injury is common in sports like football.

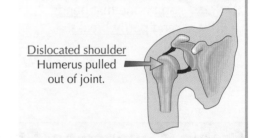

Dislocated shoulder
Humerus pulled out of joint.

Use the RICE Method to Treat Injuries

R — **REST** ➡ Stop immediately and <u>rest</u> the injury — if you carry on, you'll make it <u>worse</u>.

I — **ICE** ➡ Apply <u>ice</u> to the injury. This makes the blood vessels <u>contract</u> to reduce internal bleeding and swelling.

C — **COMPRESSION** ➡ <u>Bandaging</u> the injury will also help reduce swelling. But <u>don't</u> make it so tight that you stop the blood circulating altogether.

E — **ELEVATION** ➡ Support the limb at a <u>raised</u> level (i.e. above the heart). The flow of blood reduces because it has to work against gravity.

1) The <u>RICE method</u> is a good treatment for joint and muscle injuries like <u>sprains</u> or <u>strains</u>. It helps reduce pain, swelling and bruising.

2) As with everything, a little bit of <u>common sense</u> goes a long way. If the person has hurt their head, neck or spine — trying to elevate the injury is probably <u>not</u> a good idea.

RICE — Rest, Ice, Compression, Elevation...

Your joints can get injured if you use them too much without giving them time to recover in between. Sudden stresses can sprain ligaments, tear cartilage or even dislocate joints. You can use the RICE method to help reduce the pain and the swelling that goes along with sprains and strains.

Injuries — Types and Treatment

You need to know four different types of <u>fracture</u> and how to treat some other common injuries that you might come across when doing physical activity. Remember, if you're doing a WJEC course you don't need to know this stuff.

Bones can Break in Different Ways

1) A <u>fracture</u> is a <u>break</u> in a bone. They're usually accompanied by <u>bruising</u> and <u>swelling</u>.
2) This is because a fracture also damages the <u>blood vessels</u> in or around the bone.
3) They'll also cause a lot of <u>pain</u> because of the damaged <u>nerves</u> inside the bone.
4) There are <u>four</u> types of fracture you need to know:

In a <u>simple</u> or <u>closed</u> fracture it all happens <u>under</u> the skin. The skin itself is alright.

In a <u>compound</u> or <u>open</u> fracture the skin is torn and the bone pokes out.

<u>Greenstick fractures</u> happen in young or <u>soft</u> bone that <u>bends</u> and <u>partly breaks</u>.

A '<u>stress fracture</u>' is a small <u>crack</u> in a bone. It's caused by <u>continuous</u> stress over a <u>long period</u> of time. All other bone fractures are caused by a <u>sudden stress</u>.

Cramp, Concussion, Stitch — other Common Problems

CRAMP	<u>SYMPTOMS</u>:	<u>Involuntary</u> contraction of a muscle caused by a lack of <u>salt</u> minerals in the blood, or by a lack of blood flowing to a muscle. It's painful, but easy to treat.
	<u>TREATMENT</u>:	Just <u>stretch</u> the muscle and hold it like that, <u>massaging</u> it gently, until the muscle relaxes.

WINDING	<u>SYMPTOMS</u>:	Difficulty in <u>breathing</u>, pain in the abdomen, and you might feel sick. It's caused by a <u>blow</u> to the abdomen.
	<u>TREATMENT</u>:	Stop exercising, lean forward, and rub the affected area.

STITCH	<u>SYMPTOMS</u>:	A sharp pain in your side or abdomen. It's caused by the <u>diaphragm</u> cramping, so it can make breathing difficult.
	<u>TREATMENT</u>:	Stop exercising, take deep breaths, and breathe out slowly.

CONCUSSION	<u>SYMPTOMS</u>:	Unconsciousness, disorientation and memory loss. It's caused by a <u>blow</u> to the head.
	<u>TREATMENT</u>:	If unconscious, place the person in the <u>recovery position</u> (in this position, the head is tilted so that the airway won't be blocked by the <u>tongue</u> or by <u>vomit</u>) and get an ambulance. If they're conscious, keep the casualty under observation for 24 hours.

SHOCK	<u>SYMPTOMS</u>:	Pale, clammy skin. Rapid, weak pulse and breathing. The casualty may feel weak, faint, sick, dizzy or thirsty. It's caused by a drop in <u>blood pressure</u>.
	<u>TREATMENT</u>:	Call an ambulance, try to stop any external bleeding, reassure them and place them in the <u>recovery position</u>.

HYPOTHERMIA	<u>SYMPTOMS</u>:	Body temperature falls <u>below</u> 35 °C. Muscles go rigid, heart beats irregularly, casualty may fall unconscious.
	<u>TREATMENT</u>:	Steadily <u>raise</u> body temperature to 37 °C. Put them into <u>warm, dry clothing</u> or wrap them in a blanket. Give them <u>hot drinks</u>, and maybe a <u>warm bath</u>.

Warm-Up and Worked Exam Questions

Warm-Up Questions

1) What should you do if someone gets injured in a physical activity?
2) Name two types of soft tissue injury.
3) What is inflammation?
4) Name a joint injury caused by overuse.
5) What does RICE stand for?
6) What is the difference between an open fracture and a closed fracture?
7) What should you do if you get a stitch?

Worked Exam Questions

Work carefully through the questions below, making sure you understand them. Then move on to the practice questions on the next page. It's not too late to have another flick through the last few pages.

1   Many sports performers suffer from injuries during their careers.

   a)   Explain the difference between a sprain and a strain.

   A sprain is a joint injury where a ligament is stretched or torn.

   A strain is a tear in a muscle or tendon.

   (2 marks)

   b)   Explain how you would treat a strain.

   Rest the injury, apply ice to it, apply compression using a bandage

   and elevate the injured body part so that it is higher than the heart.

   Don't just say RICE — say what you would actually do.   *(4 marks)*

2   Many professional football players plant their studs in the ground and try to turn as they kick the ball. Name and describe **one** type of injury this movement could cause.

   It could cause a dislocation — where the bone is pulled out

   of its normal position.   *It could also cause a sprain or torn cartilage.*

   (2 marks)

3   What is tendonitis?
   Explain how an athlete could reduce the risk of developing this injury.

   Tendonitis is a condition where tendons become inflamed and sore.

   It's mainly caused by overuse, so you reduce the risk of developing it

   by allowing enough time to rest between exercise sessions.

   (3 marks)

Exam Questions

1 Which of the following **best** describes tennis elbow?

    A   A sprain

    B   An inflammation

    C   A fracture

    D   A dislocation

(1 mark)

2 George has fractured his leg.

    a)   What is a fracture?

        ....

(1 mark)

    b)   Describe the difference between a compound fracture and a greenstick fracture.

        ....

        ....

        ....

(4 marks)

3 Rosie is completing her Duke of Edinburgh Award. She camped out with her group overnight in freezing conditions.

    a)   Name the condition the group are at risk of developing.
        Describe the symptoms of this condition.

        ....

        ....

        ....

(3 marks)

    b)   Explain how Rosie should treat someone in the group who is suffering from this condition.

        ....

        ....

(3 marks)

4 Describe the symptoms of concussion and the treatment for it.

    ....

    ....

    ....

(5 marks)

Revision Summary — Section Four

Another section almost out of the way — at least this one had loads of blood and gore to keep your head off the desk. Some of it could even be useful some day — when someone's unconscious, you'll be glad you worked your way through it... So what are you waiting for... As always, keep going through them till you can answer every question without cheating.

1) What does PAR-Q stand for?

2) Give two health checks you should do before exercise.

3) Write down three ways to test cardiovascular fitness.

4) Write down four tests for health-related fitness. Say what component of fitness each one tests.

5) How can you test a) agility, b) balance, c) coordination?

6) What does the Sargent jump test measure? How do you do it?

7) What are the five principles of training?

8) Explain why rest and recovery are important.

9) What does FITT stand for? Explain what each letter means.

10) Why is it important to warm up before and cool down after exercise?

11) Describe some of the factors you need to think about when you are designing a training plan.

12) Is weight training an aerobic or anaerobic activity?

13) What percentage of your maximum heart rate should you be at when doing continuous training?

14) Describe fartlek training.

15) Describe how circuit training works.
    Is it made up of aerobic activities, anaerobic activities or both types of activity?

16) Give one advantage of doing cross training.

17) What is plyometric training used to improve?

18) Describe interval training.

19) Describe three different types of flexibility training.

20) Explain how altitude training can improve an athlete's cardiovascular endurance.

21) What are the three stages of training for a competitive athlete whose sport is seasonal?

22) What is the 'target zone' for doing aerobic training and what are 'training thresholds'?

23) Describe five different characteristics of a skilful movement.

24) List five different examples of fundamental motor skills.

25) What is the difference between an open and a closed skill?

26) Give three different ways you can learn a new skill. Explain each one.

27) Explain the difference between variable practice and fixed practice.

28) List six ways of developing a skill.

29) Explain the difference between intrinsic and extrinsic feedback.

30) Describe the difference between 'knowledge of performance' and 'knowledge of results'?

31) Name three different ways you can receive guidance and feedback.

32) What's the difference between intrinsic and extrinsic motivation?

33) What do the letters in SMART stand for? Explain what each one means.

34) Give three ways fatigue and stress can affect your skill level.

35) Describe how can you prevent injuries a) before an activity, b) during an activity,
        c) after an activity.

36) What is muscle atrophy?

37) What's the RICE method?

38) What is a stress fracture? What causes it?

39) Describe the symptoms and treatment of a) cramp, b) concussion, c) shock.

Leisure Time and Access to Facilities

You get to do what <u>you</u> want in leisure time, instead of doing chores and stuff — it's <u>great</u>. People now have <u>way more leisure time</u> than they used to — so they tend to have more time for <u>physical activity</u> too.

Leisure Time and Recreation are about Wants, not Needs

Most of our time is taken up by things that <u>need to be done</u>:

1) <u>Social</u> duties — going to school or work, and doing chores and things.

2) <u>Bodily</u> needs — mainly eating and sleeping.

In the time that's left, we can choose what we want to do. This is our <u>leisure time</u>.

> **Leisure** is <u>free time</u>, that you can use to do what you want. It might include a physical activity or sport.

Loads of people spend their leisure time doing some kind of <u>recreation</u>.

> **Recreation** is something you do in your <u>leisure time</u> to <u>relax</u> or be active.

<u>DIFFERENCES BETWEEN SPORT AND PHYSICAL RECREATION:</u>

1) Sports are more <u>competitive</u> — they have <u>rules</u>, and the aim is always to <u>win</u>. Sports have organised <u>events</u> and <u>competitions</u>.

2) Physical recreation and leisure activities are often <u>non-competitive</u> activities. You usually take part because of <u>intrinsic</u> rather than <u>extrinsic</u> motivations (see p80), e.g. you enjoy doing it. They're part of a <u>healthy, active lifestyle</u>, and are a way of keeping up a sport or physical activity <u>throughout your life</u>.

People Have More and More Leisure Time

<u>Leisure time is increasing</u> — people have <u>loads</u> more than they did fifty years ago due to:

> 1) <u>Less time working</u> — the average working week is much shorter, and holidays are longer.
> 2) <u>Technology helping with household chores</u> — e.g. washing machines, vacuum cleaners, dishwashers. These machines have gradually become better, cheaper and more widely available.

This means people have more time to spend doing physical activity, and with the extra time to practise, their <u>performance</u> will generally be better too.

As people's leisure time <u>increases</u>, so does the <u>demand</u> for facilities and services to help fill that time. There's been <u>huge growth</u> in the 'leisure industry' in recent years — and it's likely to continue.

Both the Public and Private Sectors Provide Facilities

<u>PUBLIC SECTOR FACILITIES</u>:

1) Owned by <u>local authorities</u> and <u>councils</u>.

2) Usually run at a loss (<u>funded by taxes</u>).

3) Examples include: sports pitches, leisure centres, swimming pools and sports halls.

Sometimes local authorities will try to <u>encourage</u> certain <u>groups</u> to take part in physical activities — with things like <u>special prices</u> for <u>OAPs</u>, or <u>mother-and-baby sessions</u>.

These groups are called 'priority groups', 'user groups' or 'target groups'.

<u>PRIVATE SECTOR FACILITIES</u>:

1) Owned by <u>companies</u> or <u>individuals</u>.

2) Usually run to <u>make money</u>.

3) Examples include: sports stadiums (e.g. Wembley), tennis clubs, golf clubs, and health clubs.

4) They could also be <u>voluntarily-run facilities</u>, e.g. rugby clubs, or church halls.

5) <u>National governing bodies</u> for different sports will also fund facilities and training to try to find the next sports stars.

More free time? — Not until you've finished revising...

There are loads more leisure activities available today than there were 50 years ago . You can choose to do any activity you like, as long as you can find the right facilities — more about that on the next page.

Leisure Time and Access to Facilities

Your choice of <u>leisure activities</u> can be affected by lots of different factors.

Where You Live Affects the Activities You Can Do

Your <u>location</u> will affect the physical activities you choose to do.

Facilities

You might not need <u>good facilities</u> for many physical activities — but it definitely makes playing them <u>easier</u>. There are two sorts of facilities:

OUTDOOR FACILITIES
These facilities include <u>pitches</u> (e.g. for cricket), <u>tracks</u> (e.g. athletics) and <u>facilities for water sports</u>.

INDOOR FACILITIES
These facilities are usually <u>purpose-built buildings</u> such as <u>swimming pools</u> and <u>sports halls</u> (used for loads of sports, like tennis, basketball, badminton and football).

Transport

1) It's no good having great exercise facilities if you can't get anywhere <u>near</u> them.
2) Having <u>easy access</u> to sporting facilities means you're <u>more likely</u> to use them.
3) If the facilities aren't near by, you'll need access to <u>transport</u> to get there — having a <u>car</u>, or <u>good bus links</u> to the facilities can really help.

Environment

The <u>environment</u> and <u>terrain</u> where you live will affect the activities you chose as well. If you live somewhere hilly like the Lake District, there's a huge amount of <u>opportunity</u> to do <u>outdoor activities</u> like hillwalking, mountain biking, rock-climbing or windsurfing. Because there's more opportunity, you're <u>more likely</u> to do these activities than someone who lives in the sprawling metropolis of Manchester.

Weather

The <u>weather</u> will affect your choices too.

1) If it's <u>cold</u> and <u>wet</u> outside, you're more likely to choose an <u>indoor</u> activity like badminton than go and play volleyball on the beach.
2) In <u>hot</u>, <u>humid</u> weather, you'll probably prefer a nice <u>refreshing</u> swim. <u>Pollution</u> in big cities might <u>put you off</u> doing outdoor activities too.

The <u>environment</u> can also have a big effect on your <u>performance</u> too.

1) If the <u>weather</u>'s hot and humid you'll overheat faster and won't be able to perform as well.
2) If you're exercising at <u>high altitude</u>, you breathe in less oxygen, so you'll get <u>tired</u> more quickly (see p66).
3) The <u>terrain</u> can make a difference too — running 10 km will take you longer on a <u>hilly route</u> than a <u>flat</u> one.

I like running — but only when it's sunny...

Where you live has a big impact on your choice of leisure activities. Whether there are good facilities that are easy to get to, the weather and the local environment can all affect which sports people play.

Influences on Participation

People can have an influence on the sports you take part in, whether it's your friends' opinions, your family's support or your own personal beliefs.

People Influence the Physical Activity You Do

Support from Your Family	1) Parents might encourage their children to take up sports. 2) Some sports need special clothing or equipment. It's usually parents who pay for it. 3) Many children can't easily get to and from sporting activities. They often rely on their parents to get them there.
Peer Pressure	1) Most people have a group of friends they spend most of their free time with. This group of friends is their peer group. 2) The attitudes of your friends will probably influence whether you like sport, and the sports you play. If all your mates play and like football, you'll probably play and like football. If your mates say that sport is rubbish and don't play it, you'll probably do less sport.
Role Models	People who excel in their sport can become role models for their sport and inspire people to be like them. This encourages more people to participate in their physical activity.

Race, Religion and Ethnicity can Affect Your Choices Too

1) Sometimes religious beliefs or cultural background can influence the physical activity you do.

E.g. Many Muslim women keep their bodies covered up. This may mean they're less likely to participate in activities such as swimming because of the clothing that's expected to be worn.

2) Some religious groups organise their own sporting activities for members of their community or church — like football teams or cricket matches. This also makes their church more accessible to people in the local community, and might get them more involved with the church.

3) A lot of work has been done to try and make sure that people of all races have equal opportunities in sport and physical activity. However, some studies show that UK ethnic minorities are still less likely to participate in physical activity at all levels than white people.

4) Racism and racial abuse used to be a huge problem in sport. Campaigns against racism, such as the Show Racism the Red Card campaign, have helped to bring the problem of racism into the media. Unfortunately, incidents of racial abuse still go on, e.g. racist chanting at football matches.

Racial discrimination has affected sports all over the world — the apartheid system in South Africa banned black people from playing sport with white people. As a result of this, South Africa wasn't allowed to enter many international sporting events, including the Olympics — the 1992 Olympic Games in Barcelona were the first it was allowed to enter since 1960.

We're all under the influence...

Your parents, friends, role models and your religion can all influence which sports you choose to play. Make sure you learn how each factor can affect what activities people choose to do.

Influences on Participation

There used to be a lot of <u>stupid</u> and <u>bigoted</u> views that stopped female participation in sport — held by both men <u>and</u> women. We've come on a long way, but things <u>still</u> aren't equal.

Women Used to be Discouraged From Doing Sport

Compared to nowadays, people used to think very <u>differently</u> about women in sport.

1) People thought physical activity was something to be done by <u>men only</u> and that it made women look very <u>unattractive</u>.

2) They believed that women could <u>harm themselves</u> by doing too much physical activity.

3) It was also thought women should wear 'respectable' clothing that covered their bodies up (e.g. long dresses). This meant that playing sport was very <u>uncomfortable</u>.

4) And to top it all off, people used to think women should look after the <u>home</u> and the <u>children</u> — this meant they didn't have the <u>time</u> or <u>energy</u> to play sport.

Women's Sport Tends to Have a Lower Profile

Attitudes to women in sport are much better today. More and more women are playing sport because they aren't being held back. <u>Local authorities</u> often have <u>women-only</u> evenings at gyms and swimming pools to encourage women to join in. Despite all this progress, women's sport still faces problems.

PROBLEMS FACING WOMEN'S SPORT:

1) Many sports are still considered 'male only'.

2) Women are often <u>not allowed</u> to <u>compete</u> with men. This is even true in sports like <u>snooker</u> where factors like physical strength have no relevance. Showjumping is one of the few events where women <u>can compete</u> against men.

3) <u>Poor media coverage</u> — women's events usually have a <u>lower profile</u> than men's events.

4) <u>Less sponsorship</u> — companies want to sponsor the events with the most media attention, which are generally the men's events.

5) <u>Less prize money</u> — women's events usually have less prize money than men's events, even in sports where the women do get good media coverage.

6) <u>Fewer role models</u> for women — again, lack of media support is the main problem.

Women's Sport is Now Promoted

The UK <u>WOMEN'S SPORTS FOUNDATION</u> was set up in 1984. It aims to:

1) <u>Increase awareness</u> of the issues surrounding women in sport.

2) Help girls and women to get involved in sport at <u>all levels</u>.

3) Encourage <u>organisations</u> to improve sporting <u>opportunities</u> for women.

4) Challenge <u>inequality</u> in sport and seek to bring about <u>change</u>.

5) Raise the <u>profile</u> of British sportswomen.

Women Now Have More Opportunities in Sport

1) <u>Attitudes</u> to women in sport have changed over the last 25 years. Women now have more <u>equality</u>.

2) Women can now be <u>officials</u>, like <u>referees</u> and <u>umpires</u>.

3) Female <u>managers</u> and <u>directors</u> are more common — even in <u>male-dominated sports</u> like football.

4) <u>Sports teams</u> and <u>gyms</u> that are <u>only</u> for women are getting more girls <u>involved</u> in sport.

Influences on Participation

What your <u>body can do</u> can limit the physical activities you can do (that's not exactly the shock of the century). Whether it's your <u>age</u>, your <u>health</u> or a <u>disability</u>, it all has an effect...

*Your **Age** can **Limit** the Activities You Can Do*

1) Some sports are more <u>popular</u> than others with particular age groups.
2) Most people aged 16-30 have <u>loads of choice</u> for physical activity, but more will choose to play tennis, say, rather than something like bowls.
3) People over 50 are often more <u>physically limited</u> in the sports they can choose. They tend to do <u>less strenuous</u> activities like walking or swimming.
4) Some sports such as <u>weightlifting</u> and <u>long-distance running</u> can potentially <u>damage</u> a <u>young person's</u> body. Competitions in such activities often have a <u>minimum age restriction</u>.

Poor Health May Limit the Activities You Can Do

1) Becoming <u>temporarily</u> or <u>permanently ill</u> or <u>injured</u> can <u>stop</u> you from being able to do some physical activities.
2) However, some physical activities can actually <u>help</u> with particular medical conditions, e.g. <u>swimming</u>.

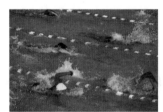

- Swimming is thought to be one of the best forms of exercise for <u>asthma sufferers</u>.

  Some <u>asthma attacks</u> are brought on by breathing in <u>cold</u>, <u>dry air</u> during physical activity. The atmosphere at a swimming pool is usually <u>warm and damp</u>, so sufferers are less likely to have an attack while exercising.
- Swimming's also a great way of exercising for people who have <u>joint problems</u> — the water helps <u>support</u> the body, which puts <u>less pressure</u> on the joints.

Disability will Influence You Too

1) Having a <u>disability</u> can limit the physical activities you can do.
2) The <u>opportunities</u> in sport and <u>access to sporting facilities</u> for disabled people used to be few and far between.
3) Nowadays, there are many schemes set up to give disabled people more opportunity to exercise and take part in activities within their physical limits.
4) Disabled sporting events are now given a lot more <u>media coverage</u> than they once were, e.g. the Paralympics are now given extensive <u>media coverage</u>, like the Olympics.
5) This media coverage is helping to <u>change people's attitudes</u> towards disability and sport.
6) It's also helping create many more <u>disabled role models</u> (like <u>Dame Tanni Grey-Thompson</u> and <u>Oscar Pistorius</u>), which encourages more disabled people to get active.

Age, health, disability — more influences for you to learn...

Age-wise it's not like you get to 50 and that's the end of the road. The oldest Olympic medallist was a Swedish chap who won a silver medal for shooting at the age of 72. Not bad if you ask me. Make sure you know how age, health and disabilities can all affect someone's participation in sport.

Influences on Participation

School, school, school... the best days of your life, so they say.

PE Teachers Can Affect Your Attitude Towards Exercise

1) A <u>good</u> teacher can build up your <u>confidence</u>, identify your <u>strengths</u> and <u>potential</u>, make activities <u>enjoyable</u> and provide <u>quality coaching</u> — whereas a bad teacher can put you off PE for life.

2) PE teachers who run <u>after-school</u> or <u>lunchtime clubs</u> are trying to <u>encourage</u> you to get more involved in sports — and they're making an effort too.

3) Your school should <u>promote</u> and give you the chance to get <u>involved</u> in <u>health awareness programmes</u>.

And Your School Facilities Have an Influence Too

1) It's not just PE teachers that affect your <u>enthusiasm</u> — your school's <u>facilities</u> make a big difference too.

2) If your school has a <u>wide range</u> of <u>good quality facilities</u> (like a gym, swimming pool, all-weather pitches and playing fields), then you'll have lots of <u>opportunities</u> to try <u>different activities</u>. The more activities you try, the more likely you are to find ones you <u>like</u>, or are <u>really good at</u>.

3) Unfortunately, not all schools have these lovely facilities. A <u>lack</u> of <u>space</u> or <u>money</u> could mean you're <u>restricted</u> to one measly, molehill-ridden field, with everyone in school wanting to use it at once.

4) But even if your school doesn't have many <u>facilities</u> itself, it can still give you <u>opportunities</u> to try <u>new sports</u> by organising <u>trips</u> to places such as dry ski slopes, ice rinks or outdoor activity centres.

Links with Clubs can give more Opportunities

1) If your school has a <u>link</u> with a club (e.g. a <u>football club</u>), it can give you <u>access</u> to <u>professional coaching</u> and the chance to get even more <u>involved</u> with the sport.

2) Getting involved with a <u>local club</u> can give you the chance to try out <u>new things</u> — you might be able to <u>coach</u> a <u>junior team</u>, or help <u>organise</u> club events. This sort of thing might also help you to have a <u>career</u> in sport.

3) Links with a club might also mean you're able to <u>train</u> for <u>qualifications</u> that you wouldn't be able to through your school.

There are Loads of Different Pathways to Follow

1) <u>Performing</u> isn't the only way to take part in sporting activities — you can be a <u>leader</u>, a <u>coach</u>, an <u>organiser</u>, a <u>choreographer</u> or an <u>official</u>. You can also get involved by <u>volunteering</u> (see p5).

2) You can't just turn up one day and expect to be made the referee — you have to <u>work towards it</u>. But you can start doing this through your <u>school</u> or a <u>club</u>.

3) There are lots of different <u>pathways</u> you can take. A pathway is a set of <u>steps</u> showing how you can <u>progress</u> through a sport, from a <u>beginner</u> to <u>competition level</u> (or <u>official</u> etc.). At each step, there are more <u>complex</u> and <u>challenging tasks</u> you have to complete.

4) In some activities, these pathways can lead to <u>official qualifications</u>, <u>accreditations</u> or <u>awards</u>.

5) A typical pathway might look something like this:

1) Doing an activity or sport regularly. → 2) Taking part in school or community sporting events. → 3) Reaching a really high standard of performance, and entering national competitions.

OR

3) Deciding to become a coach or official and working towards accreditation.

Other Factors that Affect the Sports We Choose

There are lots of other factors that influence whether or not people <u>participate</u> in particular sports.

Other Things Affect the **Sports** we **Choose**

1) Politics

E.g. the Government might use a <u>campaign</u> to promote healthy, active lifestyles, or it might provide <u>funding</u> to build a new sports facility. It also decides which sports are taught in <u>schools</u>.

2) Acceptability

Some sports are considered <u>socially unacceptable</u> by some people — e.g. they might object to off-road driving due to <u>environmental concerns</u>, or horse racing for <u>animal welfare</u> reasons.

3) Challenge/Danger

Many people are attracted to sports with an element of <u>risk</u>, like rock-climbing or motor racing. They wouldn't get the same <u>stimulation</u> and enjoyment from something like bowls.

4) Money

Learning an activity like <u>skiing</u> isn't easy for most people in this country. Sports like this are more popular with <u>wealthy</u> people who can afford to <u>go abroad</u> to ski. Similarly, some sports require <u>expensive equipment</u> which a lot of people can't afford.

5) Lifestyle

If you have a <u>sedentary lifestyle</u> (i.e. you don't do much <u>physical exercise</u>), you're more likely to choose a sport that isn't very <u>strenuous</u>. A sedentary lifestyle increases the risks of health problems such as <u>heart disease</u> or even <u>obesity</u> (see p42).

6) Skill

You'll often enjoy a sport more if you're <u>good</u> at it, or if you want to <u>improve</u>.

7) Status

Some sports have a higher <u>social status</u> than others — e.g. <u>polo</u> is often associated with the <u>wealthy</u> and 'upper class', while a <u>cheaper</u> activity like <u>football</u> is considered more 'working class'.

Money and status?

Make sure you know all the different <u>factors</u> that affect <u>participation</u>. Cover this page and see how many factors you can scribble down from memory, then check to see how many you got right.

Warm-Up and Worked Exam Questions

Warm-Up Questions

1) What is leisure?
2) Give two reasons why people have more leisure time now than they did fifty years ago.
3) What is recreation? Name one recreational activity.
4) Give two examples of a 'priority group'.
5) List seven things that influence the sports we choose to take part in.
6) How can teachers influence your attitude towards exercise?
7) Describe one career pathway you could follow to become an official.

Worked Exam Questions

You know what to do — get warmed up here, then over to the next page for some more exam-style fun.

1   Schools play a big role in encouraging participation in physical activities.

   a)   Name **two** roles in sport (besides playing) that you may be able to try at school.

   Official and coach   *There are loads of possible answers —*
                           choreographer, linesman, captain, etc...
                                                                    (2 marks)

   b)   Give **one** way that school facilities can influence participation in physical activities.

   The larger the range of facilities, the more likely students are to find

   an activity they enjoy doing, and so the more likely they'll participate.

   There are loads of answers you could give, but you only need to put one to get the mark.   *(1 mark)*

   c)   Describe **one** other way that schools can encourage participation in physical activities.

   Create links with local clubs to provide more opportunities for

   students to do different and interesting physical activities.

                                                                    (1 mark)

2   Evaluate the influences that may affect women's participation in physical activity.

   Women have fewer female role models to inspire them to do an

   activity. Women may have less access to traditionally male sports,

   e.g. rugby, and may be more likely to participate in sports they have

   more access too. The availability of 'Women only' classes may also

   encourage participation.

                                                                    (3 marks)

   If you're asked to evaluate something, that means you need to give
   the pros and cons — otherwise you won't get all the marks.

Exam Questions

1   Which of these people would be part of your peer group?

    A   Your grandparents

    B   Your parents

    C   Your teacher

    D   Your school friends

(1 mark)

2   Describe the difference between sport and physical recreation.

....

....

(2 marks)

3   John is 60 and plays badminton often.

    a)   Why might John have a lot of leisure time?

    ....

    (1 mark)

    b)   How might his age affect the sport he plays?

    ....

    (1 mark)

    c)   Discuss **two** other factors that might have affected John's choice of sport.

    ....

    ....

    ....

    ....

    (4 marks)

4   A marathon runner trains for six months before a race. Discuss how different
    environmental factors might affect the runner's performance during the race.

....

....

....

....

(3 marks)

Government Schemes

The <u>Government</u> doesn't want a country filled with obese heart disease victims.
That's why it sets up <u>schemes</u> and <u>initiatives</u> to get young people more active.

Government Schemes Encourage Physical Activity

1) The Government believes that schools have an important role to play in generating <u>interest in sport</u> — if you <u>enjoy</u> sports at school you're more likely to take them up when you leave.

2) The <u>National Curriculum</u> for PE sets out what teachers must teach. It's designed to <u>encourage</u> young people to enjoy sports, both <u>in</u> and <u>out</u> of school, and to understand that physical activity is a vital part of a <u>healthy, active lifestyle</u>.

3) PE lessons are supposed to help you develop a wide <u>range of skills</u> like <u>tactics</u>, <u>planning</u>, <u>goal setting</u> and <u>decision-making</u>, as well as improving your <u>physical skills</u>.

4) You should also have the chance to try out roles other than performing, such as <u>leading</u> or <u>officiating</u>.

5) By developing the <u>skills</u> and learning about the <u>processes</u> and <u>decisions</u> made by people in different roles (see p4-5) you're more likely to stay <u>interested</u> and <u>keep doing</u> an activity.

6) In addition to the National Curriculum, the Government has also produced schemes like <u>PESSCL</u>, <u>PESSYP</u> (see next page) and the <u>Healthy Schools Policy</u> (see below). These <u>set out in detail</u> the Government's plans for getting young people healthy and active.

The Healthy Schools Policy and PSHE Teach about Health

The <u>Healthy Schools Policy</u> is a scheme set up by the <u>Government</u> as part of the national health agenda. It tries to encourage pupils to have a <u>healthy, active lifestyle</u>. It teaches you about <u>eating healthily</u>, <u>exercise</u> and your <u>emotional needs</u>, so you can make informed decisions about your lifestyle. Different bits of the policy are taught in lessons like <u>PE</u>, <u>Food Technology</u> and <u>PSHE</u>.

Healthy Eating

1) Schools should encourage you to <u>eat healthily</u>. As well as providing <u>healthy food</u> at lunch and breaktime, they should also <u>teach</u> you about <u>balanced diets</u>.

2) The <u>Whole School Food Policy</u> means that <u>everyone</u> (parents, staff and students) is involved in planning <u>healthy meals</u>.

3) You also need to know about <u>health initiatives</u> — like eating <u>five</u> portions of <u>fruit</u> and <u>veg</u> every day.

Physical Activity

1) Schools are supposed to <u>promote physical activity</u>.

2) You must have <u>two hours</u> of <u>structured physical activity</u> a week (i.e. your PE lessons) but you should really aim to do <u>one hour</u> of <u>physical activity</u> or <u>sport</u> a day.

3) Your school should encourage you to take part in <u>extracurricular sports</u>.

Emotional Health and Well-being

1) Schools have to consider <u>vulnerable students</u> (ones who might need more <u>support</u> because of their <u>gender</u>, <u>race</u>, <u>religion</u>, <u>disability</u>, <u>sexuality</u> or <u>class</u>) and make sure they can have a <u>healthy, active lifestyle</u>.

2) This means schools have to make sure that <u>everyone</u> can take part in <u>PE lessons</u>, and that nobody is <u>discriminated</u> against for any reason.

3) All schools should have an <u>Anti-Bullying Policy</u> and <u>reward schemes</u> for good behaviour. A school's <u>pastoral system</u> (i.e. looking after your <u>personal</u> and <u>social well-being</u>) should be <u>confidential</u>.

Government Schemes

And there's more... <u>PESSYP</u> and <u>PESSCL</u> are the main Government strategies — and there are lots of <u>other initiatives</u> that have branched off from these.

PESSCL — PE, School Sport and Club Links Strategy

1) The <u>PESSCL strategy</u> was set up by the Government in 2003 to get <u>young people</u> doing <u>more</u> sport — a key target was to give at least <u>85%</u> of school children access to <u>two hours</u> per week of quality physical activity in school by 2008, which was actually achieved a year early, in 2007.

2) It encouraged <u>links</u> between schools and sports colleges — and funding was provided for this.

3) The PESSCL strategy also <u>supported</u> other schemes like <u>Specialist Sports Colleges</u> (SSC), the <u>gifted and talented</u> programme, <u>Step into Sport</u>, the <u>TOP LINK</u> programme, <u>School Sport Partnerships</u> (SSP) and other school, club and community <u>links</u>.

> **SPECIALIST SPORTS COLLEGES (SSC)** — schools that really <u>focus</u> on <u>PE</u> and <u>sport</u>. They're given <u>funding</u> from the Government for <u>equipment</u> and <u>facilities</u>, and are expected to work with local <u>primary schools</u> and their <u>local community</u> to help them develop sports too.

> **GIFTED AND TALENTED PROGRAMME** — a programme designed to help <u>elite young athletes</u> achieve their <u>full potential</u>. It aims to <u>identify high flyers</u> in PE and give them the <u>support</u> and <u>funding</u> they need to make it to the <u>top</u>.

> **STEP INTO SPORT** — aimed at <u>14-19</u> year olds. It encourages them to be <u>sports leaders</u> and <u>volunteers</u>, both <u>now</u> and in the <u>future</u>.

> **TOP LINK PROGRAMME** — a programme set up to develop <u>links</u> between schools. It helps <u>14-16</u> year olds set up <u>sport</u> or <u>dance festivals</u> for their <u>local primary schools</u> or <u>special schools</u>. It's supposed to develop <u>leadership</u> and <u>organisational skills</u>.

> **SCHOOL SPORT PARTNERSHIPS (SSP)** — <u>groups</u> of schools that <u>work together</u> to improve PE skills. Specialist Sports Colleges, other <u>secondary</u> schools, <u>primary</u> schools and <u>special</u> schools all <u>share resources</u> and <u>knowledge</u> — it gives children in these schools more <u>opportunities</u>.

PESSYP — PE and Sport Strategy for Young People

1) The <u>PE and Sport Strategy for Young People</u> (<u>PESSYP</u>) was set up in 2008 to replace PESSCL. It builds on the PESSCL strategy, with the same overall aims of increasing the <u>amount</u> and <u>quality</u> of sport schoolchildren do.

2) Like PESSCL, the first aim is for <u>everyone</u> aged 5-16 to have <u>two hours</u> of quality physical activity a week in school time. But in this new strategy, all 5-19 year olds should also be given the opportunity to do at least <u>three hours</u> of <u>extracurricular sport</u> every week — this is known as the '<u>Five Hour Offer</u>'. PESSYP also aims to increase <u>coaching opportunities</u> for older students.

3) New schemes set up as part of the PESSYP strategy include a <u>National School Sport Week</u>, a <u>Young Ambassadors programme</u> and a <u>National Talent Orientation Camp</u> — more of these last two on the next page...

Lots of acronyms to learn — PESSCL, SSC, SSP...

There are lots of different <u>schemes</u> on this page — make sure you know all the <u>names</u> and <u>what they do</u>. Remember, PESSYP was set up to replace PESSCL, and build on what it had started. But they all have a <u>similar purpose</u> — to get <u>young people</u> more <u>involved</u> with sport. That's the aim of the game.

Sport Organisations

One more desperately exciting page about getting young people off the sofa and doing exercise. Two organisations that do lots of stuff towards this are <u>Sport England</u> and the <u>Youth Sport Trust</u>.

Sport England *Want* **Everyone** *to get Into Sport*

1) <u>Sport England</u> is a Government organisation that <u>provides funding</u> for various sports schemes and programmes. Some of the money comes direct from the Government, some is from the National Lottery.

2) It provides funding to organisations such as UK Sport to develop promising UK sporting talent.

3) It also works closely with the Youth Sport Trust on providing sporting opportunities for young people.

4) The key aims are summarised in its motto '<u>Start</u>, <u>Stay</u> and <u>Succeed</u>' (also called 'Grow, Sustain, Excel').

> **Start**
> Increase participation in sport in order to improve the <u>health of the nation</u>, with a focus on <u>priority groups</u>.

<u>Priority groups</u> are groups of people that are known to take part in less physical activity than others, e.g. women.

> **Stay**
> <u>Keep</u> people in sport through an effective network of <u>clubs</u>, <u>sports facilities</u>, <u>coaches</u>, <u>volunteers</u> and <u>competitive opportunities</u>.

> **Succeed**
> Create opportunities for <u>talented performers</u> to achieve success.

5) The <u>Sports Council for Wales</u> (SCW) is an organisation that supports and funds sport in Wales. Its aims include getting 90% of Welsh secondary school children to do 60 minutes of activity five times a week (the <u>5 × 60 initiative</u>).

The **Youth Sport Trust** *Works to get* **Children** *Active*

1) The <u>Youth Sport Trust (YST)</u> is a <u>charity</u> that does loads of work aimed at getting children involved in sport. It is heavily involved in delivering the Government's <u>PESSYP</u> strategy. It runs a range of <u>programmes</u> to get different people involved in physical activities in different ways.

2) As well as the <u>Top Link Programme</u> (see prev. page), it runs a <u>Top Sportsability</u> programme to provide <u>opportunities</u> for <u>disabled children</u> to join in sporting activities with non-disabled children.

3) There's also the <u>Top Activity Programme</u> (also called <u>Active Kids</u>). This uses <u>less common</u> sports to encourage children to take part in <u>physical activity</u> — things like <u>cheerleading</u> and <u>martial arts</u>. This programme takes place <u>out</u> of school hours.

4) As part of PESSYP, it started the <u>Young Ambassadors programme</u> — a scheme to allow 16 and 17 year olds who are either <u>really good</u> at sport or have good <u>leadership skills</u> to act as <u>role models</u> for younger athletes.

5) Also as part of the new PESSYP, it runs an annual <u>National Talent Orientation Camp</u> (NTOC) for <u>gifted and talented</u> athletes. It's a camp where young athletes get to <u>train</u> and meet successful sporting <u>role models</u>, like <u>Olympic medallists</u>.

The Government funds lots of schemes to get people playing sport...

You'll be delighted to know that there's no more stuff on sports schemes and initiatives after this page. So just make sure you know the ins and outs of the various <u>Government</u> schemes, what organisations are involved in delivering them, and where all the money comes from.

Levels of Participation in Sport

You can <u>take part</u> in a sport at <u>different levels</u> — from being forced, kicking and screaming, to do it in PE at school to <u>dedicating your life</u> to it and winning an Olympic gold medal.

The **Sports Participation Pyramid**...

Not every footballer in the world is making millions playing in the Premier League.

There are <u>four different levels</u> of participation within a sport, and the <u>number</u> of people participating gets <u>smaller</u> at each increasing level. You can show this using a <u>pyramid</u>:

Stage 1 — Foundation

1) You may not <u>understand</u> all the <u>rules</u> at this stage. You'll be developing <u>basic skills</u> needed for the sport.

2) Most people are normally at this level while at <u>school</u>.

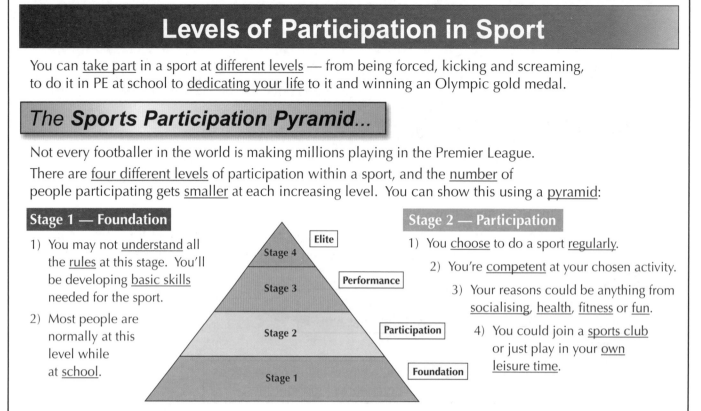

Stage 2 — Participation

1) You <u>choose</u> to do a sport <u>regularly</u>.

2) You're <u>competent</u> at your chosen activity.

3) Your reasons could be anything from <u>socialising</u>, <u>health</u>, <u>fitness</u> or <u>fun</u>.

4) You could join a <u>sports club</u> or just play in your <u>own</u> <u>leisure time</u>.

Stage 3 — Performance

1) This is when you're <u>training seriously</u> and are <u>committed to improving</u> your <u>sport-related skills</u>.

2) This might mean playing for a team or club where you receive some <u>coaching</u>.

3) You're able to <u>perform</u> and <u>compete</u> at a club or <u>regional level</u>.

Stage 4 — Elite

1) Right at the top of the pyramid are the <u>highly-skilled</u> elites who have reached a level of <u>excellence</u>.

2) At this level you're competing in <u>national</u> and <u>international</u> competitions, and can be an <u>amateur</u> or <u>professional</u> athlete.

There are **Three** Main Types of **Competition**

A lot of sport's about competition, let's face it. These are the main ways competitions are organised:

<u>LEAGUE</u> — E.g. football divisions. Each team or player plays against <u>all</u> the others at least once (often twice — home and away). They get <u>points</u> for winning or drawing a game. The winner is the player or team with the most points at the end of the season. Leagues are a very <u>fair</u> way to run a competition, because they reward <u>consistency</u> over a long time. The trouble is they may take <u>too long</u>, and if there are too many people or teams they may have to be divided up into smaller leagues.

<u>KNOCK-OUT</u> — E.g. tennis tournaments. Knock-out competitions are played in <u>rounds</u>, with each player or team playing one game per round. They go through to the next round if they win, otherwise they're out of the competition. Knock-outs are <u>easy to organise</u> and <u>quick</u> to run, but they're not as fair as you <u>only get one chance</u>. On the other hand, they're more <u>exciting</u> to watch and take part in.

<u>LADDER</u> — E.g. squash competition ladders. The players are listed on a ladder. Each can <u>challenge</u> a player higher on the ladder, but only up to a certain number of rungs higher. If they beat them, they <u>take their place</u> on the ladder. This is no good for team sports, and can be demoralising for <u>new players</u> who must start at the <u>bottom</u>.

Some competitions are made up of a <u>mixture</u> of these — and some even have <u>qualifying stages</u> (where you have to reach a <u>certain level</u> before you even get to the <u>main competition</u>).

Sports Careers

It's dead important to know the difference between an <u>amateur</u> and a <u>professional</u>. It's all about <u>money</u> — professionals get paid but amateurs don't. You only need this page if you're doing an AQA course.

Pros do it for Money — Amateurs for Love

<u>**AMATEURS**</u> — <u>don't get paid</u> for playing sport — they do it as a <u>hobby</u> because they like it.

<u>**PROFESSIONALS**</u> — <u>get paid</u> for playing their sport — it's their <u>full-time job</u>.

1) Some sports are <u>totally amateur</u>, e.g. rowing.
2) Others have professionals and amateurs who compete <u>separately</u>, e.g. boxing.
3) Others are <u>open</u> — everyone competes against everyone else, e.g. golf.

The <u>Olympics</u> were originally only supposed to be for <u>amateurs</u>. But people started to <u>bend</u> the rules — getting paid for playing their sport, but still competing as <u>amateurs</u> so they could take part in the Olympics. It became <u>impossible</u> to decide who was a true amateur, so the word 'amateur' was dropped from the Olympic rule book. <u>Governing bodies</u> and the <u>IOC</u> (International Olympic Committee) now decide who can compete in the Olympics (see p111).

Money from <u>TV</u> companies and <u>sponsorship</u> means that professional athletes can now earn millions of pounds a year.

Shamateurs — The Paid Amateurs

Amateur athletes often want to find ways to train full-time, <u>without</u> being classed as professionals.

1) **SCHOLARSHIPS** — Colleges let athletes train <u>full-time</u> for free, without doing much actual studying.
2) **TRUST FUNDS** — Prize money is paid into a <u>trust fund</u>. Athletes can take <u>living expenses</u> from the fund during their career — and get the rest when they retire.
3) **SPONSORSHIP** — E.g. athletes get paid for wearing a company's <u>logo</u> on their clothing (see p106).
4) **'EXPENSES' PAYMENTS** — These are often much <u>more</u> than what the athletes actually spend.
5) **TOKEN 'JOBS'** — Athletes can be given '<u>jobs</u>' where they don't have to do anything, so can train full-time.
6) **GIFTS** — Things like cars could be given as <u>presents</u>, and then sold.
7) **ILLEGAL PAYMENTS** — Nothing fancy here. Just take the cash and keep <u>quiet</u>.

*You Don't Have to be an **Athlete** to Have a **Career** in PE*

If you're <u>interested</u> in PE but don't fancy being a <u>professional</u> <u>sportsperson</u>, there are other <u>careers</u> you could go for.

1) <u>PE teacher</u> (see p97)
2) <u>Coach</u> or <u>trainer</u> (see p5)
3) <u>Sports physiotherapist</u> — diagnosing sports injuries and treating them through manual therapy and exercises. Sports physiotherapists also advise people about how to avoid such injuries in the future.
4) A job in <u>sports management</u> — perhaps being involved in running schemes like the ones on pages 101-103.

Would anyone like to sponsor me?

In the olden days, most sports didn't let amateurs and professionals compete together — but <u>cricket</u> did. Amateurs were '<u>gentlemen</u>', and professionals '<u>players</u>'. The teams were usually a mix of both — but once a year they played against each other in the '<u>Gentlemen and Players</u>' match.

Sponsorship

Companies sponsor stuff to get themselves good <u>publicity</u>. The more <u>famous</u> the sport, team or individual, the more companies are willing to pay. If you're doing an Edexcel or WJEC course you can skip this page.

Everything is Sponsored, from the Team to the Ball

If people are going to <u>see</u> it, companies will slap their <u>name</u> on it, whether it's a person, team, league, stand, trophy, mascot, badge, or ball. This means big bucks for the <u>famous few</u>.

Free <u>transport</u> from WellMegaTravel Ltd

Free <u>accommodation</u> from Sleepless Nights Hotels

Free sports <u>equipment</u> from Dude Sports

<u>Event</u> and <u>league</u> paid for by WoutalBalker Computers

Free <u>clothes</u> and <u>shoes</u> from 2Kool4Skool Clothes

New <u>stand</u> paid for by Hyperfizzize Energy Drink

Sports <u>scholarship</u> courtesy of Upman College

<u>Entrance fee</u>, <u>food</u> and <u>training</u> paid for by WheatyBeat Cereals

Sponsorship can be Good for Sport

1) Sponsorship pays for full-time sportspeople to <u>train</u> and <u>compete</u> — they can focus all their time on training, and not have to worry about money or another job.

2) It also pays for <u>events</u>, <u>leagues</u> and things like <u>stadiums</u>.

3) It <u>promotes</u> development of up-and-coming sports stars — people who might have struggled to get noticed or accepted into the big leagues without a sponsor.

Sponsors get a lot out of Sponsorship Too

Why do sponsors give away all that dosh? Read on and learn their devious ways...

1) **<u>FREE ADVERTISING</u>** — See a good player using it and <u>you'll want to</u> use it.

2) **<u>IMAGE</u>** — The company becomes associated with <u>winners</u>.

3) **<u>SCHOLARSHIPS</u>** — Some <u>universities</u> and <u>colleges</u> offer places (at discounted grades) to students who excel at particular sports. In return universities gain <u>prestige</u> for sporting excellence.

4) **<u>TAX AND HOSPITALITY</u>** — Sponsors <u>don't</u> usually have to <u>pay tax</u> on the money they spend on sponsorship. They also get <u>free tickets</u> to the events they sponsor, which they can use to impress clients and employees.

5) **<u>AREN'T THEY NICE</u>** — Companies often sponsor <u>charity</u> and <u>local events</u>. Whether this is out of the kindness of their hearts or to <u>improve</u> their <u>corporate image</u> is by the by.

CGP CGP CGP CGP (CGP — Official Sponsors of page 106)...

Sponsorship is a good way of getting money into sport. On the surface, it looks like a win-win situation for everyone, but it does have downsides (see p107 for the dark side of sponsorship). Make sure you know <u>who</u> gets <u>what</u> out of it. And <u>memorise</u> all the ways that companies get their names into sport.

Sponsorship

It's not all good news when it comes to sponsorship — this page covers the <u>bad bits</u>.
If you're doing the Edexcel or WJEC courses you can skip this page too.

Sponsorship *Isn't* All Great Though

1) It could all turn nasty — get <u>injured</u>, lose your <u>form</u> or get a <u>bad reputation</u>
   and it's bye–bye sponsorship deal.

2) Abuse of power — associating cigarettes and alcohol with sport gives a <u>false</u> image of health.

3) Sometimes athletes have to fulfil <u>contracts</u> with their sponsor — they might have to turn up at a
   <u>special event</u> or appear in a <u>TV advert</u> (even if they don't want to).

4) Athletes can get into <u>trouble</u> with their sponsor if they're photographed
   using <u>another company</u>'s products.

It's Not Always *Easy* to get Sponsored

Companies don't always want to take a <u>chance</u> on people who are <u>new</u> to a sport — they want
to <u>know</u> they're putting their name on someone <u>good</u>. And if a team or sportsperson <u>can't</u> find
a sponsor, they might not be able to <u>compete</u>.

1) <u>Big companies</u> want people to <u>see</u> their <u>logos</u> — so they won't bother with <u>small</u>, <u>local teams</u> or
   sports with a <u>low profile</u>. High profile sports (like <u>football</u>) usually find it quite <u>easy</u> to get sponsored.

2) When games are going to be <u>broadcast</u> on <u>TV</u>, sponsors are <u>keen</u> to be <u>associated</u> with them,
   but often won't sponsor non-televised games.

3) <u>Local teams</u> and <u>leagues</u> are more likely to be sponsored by <u>local companies</u>, who want to get their
   <u>name</u> seen by the <u>community</u>. There can be lots of teams <u>competing</u> for sponsorship though, and
   not all of them will be lucky. They have to send out lots of <u>begging letters</u> asking for sponsorship.

4) Sometimes <u>school teams</u> get sponsored by companies whose owners have <u>children</u> in the team.
   This is good while it lasts, but the sponsorship might suddenly <u>disappear</u> when the child <u>leaves</u>.
   It might also mean that the team feels <u>obliged</u> to include the child in the team, even if there are
   better players — it could lead to <u>favouritism</u>.

5) If teams rely on sponsors from <u>previous years</u> or <u>events</u>, they could be left in a bit of a pickle
   if the sponsors <u>change their minds</u>.

Some Types of Sponsorship are *Unacceptable*

1) <u>Cigarette</u> and <u>tobacco</u> companies <u>aren't</u> allowed to sponsor sports in the EU
   — cigarettes are <u>harmful</u>, so they can't be <u>promoted</u> through sport.

2) <u>Alcoholic drinks</u> companies can <u>sometimes</u> be sponsors,
   though <u>not</u> usually for <u>youth events</u>.

3) Companies that are considered by many to promote <u>racist</u>,
   <u>sexist</u> or other <u>discriminatory views</u> aren't allowed to be sponsors.

4) <u>Unhealthy food</u> companies have to be <u>careful</u> when they
   sponsor sports — they can't suggest that their products are <u>healthy</u>
   (because they're associated with sports) if they're not.

5) Companies like <u>banks</u>, <u>sports clothes/equipment brands</u> and <u>car manufacturers</u>
   don't normally have any problems being sponsors.

*Racing cars used to be
sponsored by cigarette
manufacturers. They aren't
allowed any more because it's
seen as unacceptable.*

---

*

You're probably so used to seeing sponsors' names on things, you hardly <u>realise</u> they're there — like
<u>Barclays Premier League</u>, or the <u>Reebok Stadium</u>. It's important you know the <u>downsides</u> to sponsorship
— make sure you know what types are <u>unacceptable</u>, and why some teams <u>struggle</u> to find sponsors.

Warm-Up and Worked Exam Questions

Warm-Up Questions

1) Name four Government-funded schemes that are aimed at getting young people living healthy, active lives.

2) What are the three components of the Healthy Schools Policy?

3) What does PESSCL stand for?

4) Name the four stages of the participation pyramid.

5) In what type of competition does each team play all the others — ladder, league or knock-out?

6) What is the main difference between an amateur and a professional?

7) Not including being a sportsperson, list three careers in PE.

8) Is sponsorship good for sport, bad for sport, or a bit of both?

9) Give one example of unacceptable sponsorship.

Worked Exam Questions

Here are some more juicy worked examples to get your teeth into before heading on over to the exam questions on the next page.

1 Badminton competitions are often structured as ladder competitions.
Explain how this type of competition works.

Players are listed on a "ladder". You can challenge any player who occupies a position up to a specific number of rungs above you. If you beat them, you take their place on the ladder.

(3 marks)

2 a) Describe **two** benefits for a company of sponsoring an athlete.

The company gets advertising, and it can be good for the company's image.

(2 marks)

b) Evaluate the advantages and disadvantages of sponsorship for an athlete.

They get financial help with things like travel, accommodation, equipment and training. This might mean they can attend more events or have better equipment than they would otherwise. However the sponsors may try to dictate which events the athlete competes in, and the athlete may only be allowed to use particular products.

Make sure you write down disadvantages as well as advantages to get all the marks

(4 marks)

Exam Questions

1   According to the Government, how many hours a week **must** be spent
    doing physical activity in school?

    A   2

    B   3

    C   4

    D   5

(1 mark)

2   The diagram below shows the sports participation pyramid.

    a)   Which of the stages shown is the elite stage?

    ....

(1 mark)

    b)   Describe the elite stage of the participation pyramid.

    ....

    ....

(1 mark)

3   Sport England provides funding for sports schemes.
    Explain what is meant by its motto 'Start, Stay and Succeed'.

....

....

....

(3 marks)

4   Chris is an amateur hockey player. Suggest ways in which Chris could get the money to
    train full-time, without being classed as a professional.

....

....

....

(3 marks)

International Sport

International competitions just keep getting bigger and bigger. For the exam, you need to know about their pros and cons, and how attitudes towards them vary. If you're doing a WJEC or Edexcel course you don't need to know about this for the exam.

There are Loads of **International Sporting Events**

These include:

The Olympic Games: Summer and winter competitions held every four years.
The Pan American Games: Held every four years for countries in North, South or Central America.
The Commonwealth Games: Held every four years for countries in the Commonwealth (a group of countries that used to be in the British Empire).
World Cups: In many sports, e.g. cricket, rugby, football — every four years.

Nowadays, nearly every major sport has its own world championship.

Big International Competitions have **Pros** and **Cons**

Big tournaments sound great, and mostly they are. But, as always, there are some downsides.

Benefits

1) Players and supporters from different countries can meet, and experience different cultures and ways of life.

2) Competition between the best athletes in the world constantly pushes standards higher.

3) International events encourage people from all around the world to take part in sport.

Problems

1) Big tournaments are expensive to organise, so poor countries can't afford to stage them.

2) Not even rich countries are willing to host big competitions without help from big business — this makes sport more commercialised.

3) Some countries want success at sport to 'prove' they are more successful than an enemy. The USA and USSR used to do this.

Different Countries have Different Attitudes to Sport

Every country wants success in sport — it gives status and pride, and provides role models that will encourage people to be healthier. Different countries promote sport in different ways...

UNITED KINGDOM

1) PE is compulsory in schools.

2) Grants and sponsorship are available for promising talent.

3) Some top competitors have trust funds.

4) Various campaigns boost participation (see p101-103).

USA

1) PE is compulsory in schools.

2) School and college sport is high profile and attracts big sponsorship.

3) Scholarship schemes help promising athletes.

4) Top college athletes go into professional leagues.

FORMER EASTERN BLOC

(Countries that were dominated by the **USSR**)

1) Sport was controlled by the state.

2) Talented children were trained from a very young age — then given token jobs in the army or industry.

3) Sport has been more open since 1989.

THIRD WORLD COUNTRIES

1) Popular sport has to be cheap — football and athletics are booming.

2) International success will earn money.

3) Athletes are often given token government jobs.

International Sport

The first ever <u>Olympic Games</u> were held in 776 BC in <u>Ancient Greece</u> and they've <u>changed</u> quite a bit since then. If you're doing the Edexcel or WJEC courses you can miss this page out.

Olympic *Organisations* Keep Things *Fair*

1) The <u>International Olympic Committee</u> (IOC) is made up of members from just about all the <u>countries</u> that <u>compete</u>. They make <u>judgements</u> and <u>rules</u> to keep things <u>fair</u>. They also decide <u>where</u> the Olympics are going to be held. It's their job to <u>promote</u> the <u>Olympics</u> and the <u>Olympic spirit</u> (the Olympic spirit is believing it's more important to <u>take part</u> than <u>win</u>).

2) The <u>British Olympic Association</u> (BOA) looks after the <u>UK</u>'s involvement in the Games. It selects athletes for 'Team GB' and helps them to prepare, e.g. by organising time management and goal setting workshops.

Being a *Host City* has its *Good* and *Bad Points*

The Olympics are always hosted by a <u>city</u>, not a whole country.
<u>Hosting</u> the Games should bring only <u>advantages</u> — but it doesn't always work out like that...

Advantages

1) The host city gets added <u>prestige</u> — useful if you want to attract <u>trade</u> and <u>tourism</u>.

2) The <u>facilities</u> built for the Games can be used by the locals after the events have finished.

3) <u>Businesses</u> in the host city will do masses of <u>extra trade</u> during the Games.

4) The organisers can try to make a <u>profit</u>.

Disadvantages

1) It's getting more <u>expensive</u> to host the Games.

2) If there are problems, the organisers could <u>lose</u> enormous amounts of <u>money</u>.

3) <u>Security</u> could be a problem — <u>hooligans</u> or <u>terrorists</u> might disrupt the Games.

4) If a city's <u>infrastructure</u> (e.g. its phone or transport systems) <u>can't cope</u>, it could lead to <u>frustration</u> for locals and visitors.

The Olympic Games have had Their *Ups* and *Downs*

Since the <u>Modern Olympics</u> started in 1896, there have been quite a few <u>ups and downs</u>.

1896 in **ATHENS**
The first <u>Modern Olympic Games</u> were organised by <u>Baron de Coubertin</u>. Only men could compete.

1936 in **BERLIN**
<u>Hitler</u> wanted the Games to prove the <u>superiority</u> of white northern Europeans. But the star of the games was Jesse Owens, a black American who won <u>four golds</u>.

1972 in **MUNICH**
<u>Palestinian terrorists</u> killed two, and kidnapped nine, Israeli athletes. The hostages, five terrorists and a policeman were later killed in a failed rescue attempt.

1980 in **MOSCOW**
The USA and many other countries <u>boycotted</u> the Games (i.e. they didn't go to them) as a protest against the Soviet invasion of Afghanistan.

1984 in **LOS ANGELES**
The Games made a big <u>profit</u> — most things were sponsored by large companies. The USSR and allies <u>boycotted</u> the games in retaliation for the 1980 American boycott.

1992 in **BARCELONA**
<u>No boycotts</u>, and <u>South Africa</u> entered a team for the first time since 1960. It had been <u>banned</u> since 1964 because of its racist apartheid laws.

2008 in **BEIJING**
There were some <u>protests</u> over China's <u>human rights record</u>, but the Games went quite smoothly.

Aren't the Olympics great — well done those Ancient Greeks...

The <u>Olympics</u> are a <u>massive deal</u>, especially to the <u>host city</u>. They take years of <u>preparation</u>, and cost a lot of <u>money</u>. Make sure you can list all the <u>advantages</u> and <u>disadvantages</u> of hosting the Olympics.

Sport and the Media

There's no getting away from it — sport's there in the <u>daily papers</u>, on the <u>radio</u>, in <u>books</u>, in <u>films</u>, on the <u>internet</u>. Choose any type of <u>media</u> and it's there. Which is great if you <u>love</u> it, but not so great if you don't.

Sport turns up **Everywhere**

1) <u>TV</u> and <u>Radio</u> — most <u>major sporting events</u> will be shown on TV (<u>Wimbledon</u> takes over for two weeks every summer, and the <u>football World Cup</u> is almost unavoidable).

2) <u>Cable</u> and <u>Satellite</u> — they provide <u>special TV channels</u> dedicated to sport, and sometimes show events on a <u>pay-per-view</u> basis.

3) <u>Interactive TV services</u> — you can find out <u>results</u> and watch <u>extra coverage</u> on these.

4) <u>Internet</u> — there are some events you can watch <u>live</u> (or get <u>live commentaries</u> for) on the internet. Big teams, sports organisations and tournaments will have their own <u>websites</u>, so you can keep up-to-date with all their <u>news</u>.

5) <u>Newspapers</u> and <u>Magazines</u> — just about all newspapers have a <u>sports section</u>, with <u>recent results</u>, <u>league tables</u> and <u>general sporty news</u>. You can also buy magazines <u>dedicated</u> to <u>particular sports</u>.

6) <u>Books</u> and <u>Films</u> — examples include <u>biographies</u> about sports personalities, <u>coaching books</u> for particular sports, and films such as 'Million Dollar Baby' (which, if you've not seen it, is about boxing).

The media coverage of sport relies heavily on <u>technology</u> (see p114). Apart from making all these forms of coverage possible, it also improves them with things like <u>instant replays</u>, <u>photo finishes</u>, <u>underwater cameras</u>, <u>split times</u>, and timing to hundredths or <u>thousandths of seconds</u>.

Media Coverage Can Be **Entertaining** or **Informative**

SPORTS PROGRAMMES:
Can be for <u>entertainment</u> (like live sport, highlights or quiz shows) or <u>information</u> (like documentaries). You can also get <u>instructive</u> or <u>educational</u> programmes, like a coaching series.

SPORTS ARTICLES:
Sports results and analysis (<u>informative</u>), behind the scenes, players' private lives, biographies (<u>entertainment</u>).

The **Director** can **Influence** the **Coverage**

1) The <u>director</u> of a sports programme can <u>influence</u> your <u>opinions</u> of a sport or sportsperson.

2) Some sports can be <u>advertised</u> to make them look really <u>exciting</u> (like using <u>dramatic sound effects</u> and <u>voice-overs</u>). <u>Attractive stars</u> can also make you want to watch a particular sport.

3) The director <u>chooses</u> which bits you see — and also which bits you <u>don't</u>. If they only show the <u>reaction</u> to something, and not the <u>incident</u> that led up to it, you could form a different <u>judgement</u> than if you saw the whole thing.

4) It's possible to <u>edit interviews</u>, to make the person being interviewed come across in a <u>different light</u> — the interviewee could appear <u>more arrogant</u> or <u>less intelligent</u> than they actually are.

There are loads of ways to use the media to follow a sport ...

Make sure you know the <u>different forms</u> of <u>media</u>, and how they can show sports. <u>Be aware</u> that what you see on TV might be biased — the <u>director</u> is <u>controlling</u> what you see, and what you don't.

Sport and the Media

The <u>media</u> has lots of <u>influences</u> on modern sport — some of them are <u>good</u>, others are <u>bad</u>. You need to be able to give examples of both, and know how fashion affects sport too.

The **Media** can have a **Good Effect** on Sport...

The coverage of sport in the media does good stuff for sport.

| Money | Media companies pay for the rights to show a sport — <u>sponsorship</u> for a sport will also <u>increase dramatically</u> if it's popularised by the media.

| Education | People learn about the <u>rules and tactics</u> of sports.

| David Beckham | (OK I couldn't think of a good 'D'). Produces <u>role models</u> for people to aspire to. If the role models stay good, everything's fine.

| Inspiration | Brings sport to people who may not experience it otherwise. This can <u>encourage participation</u>.

| Aid to Coaching | Sport on TV and video lets you <u>study the performance</u> of others.

You can improve your performance by studying your own and your competitors technique.

Promotional campaigns in the media can also <u>encourage</u> people to <u>take up sports</u> and have a <u>healthy</u>, <u>active lifestyle</u>. Just before, during and after <u>Wimbledon</u>, lots of <u>tennis centres</u> run sessions to try and get <u>children</u> involved. Campaigns also use <u>famous sports stars</u> as <u>role models</u> to make children want to take up sports.

...and a **Bad Effect** on Sport

The media does lots of good for sport, but it has a <u>dark side</u> to it to.

| Bias | Only the really popular spectator sports get plenty of coverage. Very <u>little coverage</u> is given to <u>less popular sports</u>, starving them of all the benefits shown above.

| Lack of Attendance | Watching it live on telly means you're not at the game — <u>reducing ticket sales</u>, then the media 'steals' more of this money with 'pay-per-view' or channel subscription fees.

| Overload | <u>Too much sport</u> (according to some people).

| Open season | <u>Sports stars are hounded</u> by the media, who are quick to pounce if a sports superstar's halo slips.

| Demands | The media actually <u>imposes</u> rules on sports to make them <u>more exciting</u>, e.g. tie breaks were introduced into tennis, partly as a result of <u>media pressure</u> to make matches shorter.

Sports can go **In** and **Out** of **Fashion**

1) Sports or leisure activities can go <u>in</u> or <u>out</u> of <u>fashion</u>. In the 90s, aerobics became very fashionable with endless tedious celebrity fitness videos being released.

2) Sports clothing has also become a lot more fashionable. If the <u>clothing</u> or <u>equipment</u> for a physical activity is fashionable, people are more likely to do the activity.

3) Going to the <u>gym</u> is very fashionable at the moment — which has meant more gyms have opened — so people now have <u>more opportunity</u> to go to them.

Technology in Sport

For AQA or WJEC courses, you need to know how <u>science</u> and <u>technology</u> have affected sport. Some developments help athletes <u>improve</u> their <u>performance</u>, while others help keep things <u>fair</u>.

Technology helps Athletes Improve

1) Lots of the <u>technology</u> used today is designed to help athletes <u>perform better</u> at their sports.

2) <u>New materials</u> are used to make sports equipment and clothes more <u>effective</u> — from shoes to swimming costumes to tennis rackets.

3) Athletes' <u>diets</u> can be designed to <u>enhance</u> their performance, due to a better <u>scientific understanding</u> of what their bodies <u>need</u> to do well.

4) **Improvements to** <u>training facilities</u> like all-weather pitches make sport more <u>accessible</u> for everyone. Roofs on stadiums (like Centre Court at Wimbledon) mean that matches can go ahead even if it rains (which, let's face it, it probably will).

5) There have also been developments to make sports <u>safer</u>.

ICT can be used in Training

1) <u>ICT programs</u> can be used to analyse, monitor and plan training sessions.

2) Sometimes coaches will make <u>videos</u> of their athletes' training so the athletes can see for themselves how they need to <u>improve</u>. Videos can also be used to <u>track progress</u>.

3) Computer software lets you analyse <u>performance</u> and <u>training statistics</u> — things like service speeds in tennis and golf swings. A training programme can be <u>designed</u> around the <u>results</u> of the analysis so the athlete can work on <u>weak areas</u>.

4) Better technology has led to more <u>accurate timings</u> in events like sprints and cycle races — they can be measured to tiny <u>fractions</u> of a <u>second</u>, so minute improvements are noticed.

5) <u>Interactive software</u> (even things like games consoles) can be used in training, especially in <u>bad weather</u>.

Some Technology helps the Referee or Umpire

Referees and umpires have to make lots of <u>snap decisions</u> in <u>live matches</u>. Sometime it can be hard to judge, especially if they're far away from the action. Technological developments like the <u>video official</u>, <u>replays</u> and <u>photo finishes</u> help them make <u>fair judgments</u>.

<u>**CYCLOPS**</u> (<u>tennis</u>) — Cyclops is a system used at <u>Wimbledon</u> to help decide if <u>serves</u> are <u>in</u> or <u>out</u>. It's made up of <u>infrared beams</u> that lie just above the ground. If the beams are <u>broken</u> (if a serve is out), they make a 'beep'. It can make <u>mistakes</u> — but it's pretty <u>accurate</u>, and makes things a lot <u>easier</u> for the umpire (especially if the balls are travelling at over 140 mph). It's also used at big championships like the US Open and the Australian Open.

<u>**HAWKEYE**</u> (<u>cricket</u> and <u>tennis</u>) — Hawkeye was originally developed for <u>cricket matches</u>, but has since been used in <u>tennis matches</u> as well. It uses a set of six cameras to <u>track</u> and <u>predict</u> the path of the <u>ball</u>. In cricket, it's mainly used by the <u>commentators</u> to discuss the umpire's <u>lbw</u> (leg before wicket) <u>decisions</u>. In tennis, it's used for the players to <u>challenge</u> the decision of whether their shots are in or out.

I say — that's simply not cricket...

The <u>lbw</u> (leg before wicket) rule in <u>cricket</u> is a bit confusing — it's when the <u>umpire</u> decides that the ball would have hit the <u>stumps</u> (and so got the batsman <u>out</u>) if the batsman hadn't got in the <u>way</u>. It's normally down to the <u>umpire's decision</u>, but technology like <u>Hawkeye</u> can confirm if they're right.

Warm-Up and Worked Exam Questions

Warm-Up Questions

1) Media coverage only does a sport good. True or false?
2) Name one way both the UK and the USA encourage people to be healthier.
3) What is the BOA?
4) List two problems that a city might have to deal with when hosting the Olympics.
5) How might the director of a sports programme affect what is shown?
6) How does fashion affect participation in sport?

Worked Exam Questions

Here's the last set of worked examples and exam-style questions for you to have a go at.

1   Many sports have been influenced by improvements in technology.

   a)   Give **two** examples of technology that have been introduced to help officials make decisions. Name a different sport in which each technology is used.

   Cyclops — tennis   *Both types of technology are used in tennis, but*
                                the question has asked for different sports so
   Hawkeye — cricket   *make sure you think of two.*

   (4 marks)

   b)   Give an example of how each of the following can be used to help athletes train and improve their performance.

   Technology

   New materials make sports equipment and clothes perform better.

   ICT

   Allows athletes to monitor and analyse their performance.

   (2 marks)

2   Describe **three** ways that the media can influence participation in sport.

   High media coverage of a sport will help to produce role models, who

   inspire people to participate in that sport. Generally there are more

   opportunities to participate in sports made popular by the media,

   which means that people are more likely to take part in these sports.

   Sports with good media coverage tend to have more sponsorship,

   which can enable people to participate in the sport who may be unable

   to afford to otherwise.

   (3 marks)

Exam Questions

1   Which of the following is a type of educational sports programme?

     A   Live sport shows

     B   Highlights

     C   Quiz shows

     D   Documentaries

(1 mark)

2   The Olympic Games is a large international event that is held every four years.

     a)   The International Olympic Committee (IOC) is made up of members from all the countries that compete in the Games. Give **one** role of the IOC.

        ....

(1 mark)

     b)   The 2008 Olympic Games were held in Beijing, China.
        Describe **two** advantages of hosting the Olympic Games for Beijing.

        ....

        ....

(2 marks)

     c)   Suggest how top performances in Olympic Games events may increase participation in sport.

        ....

        ....

(2 marks)

3   Jack enjoys watching his favourite team play football on television.

     a)   Name **three** other forms of media that Jack could use to follow his team.

        ....

        ....

        ....

(3 marks)

     b)   The club that Jack supports is losing money because of the media coverage it receives. Explain what might be happening.

        ....

        ....

(2 marks)

Revision Summary — Section Five

Well, that's your lot — the final section is out of the way. All you have to do now is to make sure
you know it all. There are quite a lot of questions here — but like before, I wouldn't try to do them
all at once. Just take it easy at first, and you'll be storming through the lot in no time. Enjoy...

1) What's leisure time? What's recreation?
2) Give three reasons why people have more leisure time now than 50 years ago.
3) What's the difference between public sector facilities and private sector facilities?
4) Name six factors that affect the sports we choose, and explain them.
5) Explain how your family can influence which sports you do.
6) How might your religion affect the sports you do?
7) Name four problems facing women's sport today.
8) Name three things the Women's Sports Foundation does.
9) How can your age affect which physical activities you do?
10) Give an example of a type of exercise that is good for asthma sufferers.
11) Name two disabled role models.
12) Give three ways a good PE teacher can affect your attitude towards PE.
13) Give three advantages of schools forming links with sports clubs.
14) Give four ways, other than actually playing, that you could get involved in sport.
15) Outline the key requirements of the Healthy Schools policy.
16) What do PESSCL and PESSYP stand for?
17) Describe a) Specialist Sports Colleges, b) Gifted and Talented Programmes
    and c) School Sport Partnerships.
18) What is the 'Five Hour Offer'?
19) What does Sport England do? What's 'Start, Stay, Succeed' all about?
20) Name three different programmes that the Youth Sport Trust is involved in.
    Explain what each one does.
21) Name and describe the three main types of competition.
22) What's the difference between a professional and an amateur?
23) Give five ways that amateurs can get the money to afford to train full-time.
24) Name three possible sports-related careers (other than being a professional athlete).
25) Give three ways sponsorship can be good for sport.
26) Name four things sponsors get out of sponsorship.
27) Give three ways sponsorship can be bad for sport.
28) Give two types of sponsorship that are unacceptable.
29) Name three international sporting events.
30) Describe the advantages and disadvantages of hosting the Olympics.
31) Name four different types of media that feature sport.
32) Describe the good and bad effects the media has on sport.
33) How is ICT used in training sessions?
34) Describe Cyclops and Hawk-Eye.

Answering Exam Questions

You've made it to the end of the book. Now there's just the <u>tiny</u> matter of the exam left. Here's what to <u>expect</u> in your exam and some <u>exam tips</u> to help you on your way to GCSE PE victory.

In the Exam — **Read** the Questions and **Don't Panic**

1) <u>Read</u> every question <u>carefully</u>.

2) The <u>number of marks</u> each question is worth is shown in <u>brackets</u> a bit like this:

> **5** (a)   What is meant by the term 'flexibility'?   **(1)**
> ....

The number of <u>answer lines</u> is also a good guide to how much to write.

3) The number of marks is normally a <u>good guide</u> to the <u>number of points</u> you need to make in your answer.

4) It also helps you know roughly <u>how long</u> to spend on a question — you don't want to use half an hour writing an essay for one mark.

5) Make sure your answers are <u>clear</u> and <u>easy to read</u>. If the examiner can't read your handwriting, they won't be able to give you any marks.

6) <u>Don't panic</u> — if you get stuck on a question, just <u>move on</u> to the ➡ next one. You can come back to it if you have time at the end.

If you do get panicky — stop and take a <u>few deep breaths</u>. It can really help.

Your Exam is Made up of **Different Types** of Question

Multiple Choice

1) The multiple choice questions will give you a choice of <u>four</u> or <u>five</u> possible answers.
   It tells you on the paper how to answer the question — you'll either have to <u>circle</u> the answer, or put a <u>tick</u> or a <u>cross</u> in a <u>box</u>.

2) Make sure you only choose <u>one</u> answer — if you pick more than one, you won't get any marks.
   (Don't worry if you make a mistake though — you can change your answer, as long as it's clear which one you've gone for in the end.)

3) If you <u>don't know</u> the answer to a question, <u>guess</u>. You don't lose marks for a wrong answer — and if you guess, you've at least got a chance of getting it right.

Short and **Long Answer** Questions

1) <u>Short answer</u> questions are usually worth between <u>one</u> and <u>four</u> marks. <u>Long answer</u> questions are normally worth about <u>six</u> marks.

2) Make sure you <u>read the question</u> carefully. For example, if you're asked for two influences, make sure that you give <u>two</u>, otherwise you won't get all the marks.

Questions on a **Scenario** You Were Given **Before** the Exam

...but <u>only</u> if you're doing AQA

1) If you are doing AQA, you'll be given a copy of a <u>scenario</u> a few weeks before the exam.
   This is basically just a <u>story</u> about someone doing some kind of <u>physical activity</u> (or perhaps someone doing no exercise at all...).

2) <u>Read through</u> the scenario <u>really carefully</u>. Have a good think about the <u>issues</u> it raises — things like what kind of <u>training</u> the person in the story might need to do, or how they could improve their <u>diet</u>.

3) The scenario will be printed out for you in the exam paper. You'll be asked a mixture of <u>short</u> and <u>long answer</u> questions about it. Use everything you thought about <u>beforehand</u> to help you answer.

It's time for the exam — don't panic...

So — <u>read</u> the question, look at the number of <u>marks</u>, answer the question and <u>don't panic</u>. Make sure that you sleep and eat well the night before the exam, so you're in tip top condition for the big day.

Answering Exam Questions

It's not just PE those examiners want to test you on. They've included a few marks for how well you can <u>communicate</u> your answer too. It sounds tricky, but if you take care it could mean some easy marks.

Don't Forget to Watch Your **Spelling** and **Grammar**

1) Some of the questions on the exam paper will test your <u>written communication skills</u> (otherwise known as '<u>how well you can write your answer</u>') as well as your amazing PE knowledge.

2) The questions where you get marks for your communication skills will always be the <u>longer ones</u> towards the end of the paper — they're usually worth about <u>6 marks</u> each.

3) Your <u>exam paper</u> should tell you <u>which questions</u> your communication skills are being tested on.
AQA and WJEC stick a <u>list</u> on the <u>front cover</u>. Edexcel and OCR put an <u>asterisk</u> (*) next to the <u>question number</u> inside the paper. AQA also mark these questions with 'Answer in continuous prose'.

4) You can pick up some easy marks just by making sure that you do the following things.

> 1) Make sure you <u>answer the question</u> being asked — it's easy to go off on a tangent.
> 2) Make sure your answer is <u>organised</u>. It's a really good idea to have a think what you're going to cover in your answer before you start writing it. That way you can make sure you <u>structure</u> your answer well, and cover all the points you want to.
> 3) Write in <u>full sentences</u> and use correct <u>spelling</u>, <u>grammar</u> and <u>punctuation</u>.
> 4) Use the correct <u>PE terminology</u>.

EXAMPLE

15* A school wants to encourage its pupils to take more exercise outside of PE lessons.
Discuss the factors that may affect a teenager's participation in extra-curricular physical activity. **(6)**

Good answer

There are lots of factors that might affect a teenager's level of participation in extra-curricular physical activity. Some of these factors are practical, and others are social.

Participation may be limited by the availability of sports facilities in the local area. Access to facilities may be limited by local transport.

Cost may be a factor. If joining a sports club or buying equipment is too expensive, it will discourage people from taking part.

If the teachers at a school encourage pupils to take part in sports, and the school provides a variety of extra-curricular sports clubs, this may encourage pupils to participate.

A teenager's peer group can have a big influence on their choice of extra-curricular activities. If a certain sport is fashionable amongst your peers, it may encourage you to take part in that activity too.

Gender may also have an effect on which sports people take part in. Some sports are seen as traditionally 'male' or 'female'. For example, if the school started a netball club, it may find it easier to encourage girls to participate than boys.

Having an appropriate sporting role model might encourage a teenager to participate in sport. This may be a family member, like a parent, or a role model from the media, such as a famous footballer.

Bad Answer

Things which might encourage participation in sport:
• good local facilities
• local transport available
• encouragement by teachers/school
• sport being popular in your peer group
• sporting role models

Things which might stop teenagers participating in sport:
• cost
• bad local facilities
• gender — if only traditionally 'male' or 'female' sports are available.

There's nothing wrong with the PE in the bad answer, but you'd miss out on some nice easy marks just for not bothering to link your thoughts together properly or put your answer into proper sentences.

For easy marks — communicate well good...

So for the <u>long answer</u> questions, write in <u>full sentences</u> and watch your <u>spelling</u> and <u>grammar</u>. <u>Organise</u> what you want to say <u>before</u> you start writing, and those marks could be yours for the taking.

Practice Exams

Once you've been through all the questions in this book, you should feel pretty confident about the exam. As final preparation, here are two **practice exams** to get you properly set up for the real thing.

Paper 1 is a mixture of multiple choice, short and long answer questions, covering topics from all of the different sections. It's designed to give you the best possible preparation for the different question styles in the actual exams, whichever specification you're following.

Paper 2 is a series of questions that are all based around a scenario. If you're doing an AQA course, it's a brilliant way to practise for the pre-released scenario section of your exam. If you're following a different exam board, it's still a fantastic way to test your PE know-how.

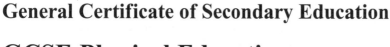

CGP   Practice Exam Paper
GCSE Physical Education

General Certificate of Secondary Education

GCSE Physical Education

Paper 1

Time allowed:
1 hour 30 minutes

Centre name				
Centre number				
Candidate number				

Surname
Other names
Candidate signature

Instructions to candidates
- Write your name and other details in the spaces provided above.
- Answer **all** questions in the spaces provided.
- Do all rough work on the paper.

Information for candidates
- The maximum mark available for this paper is **80**.
- The marks available are given in brackets at the end of each question or part-question.
- In questions 16 and 17 your communication skills will be assessed. You should answer these questions in continuous prose and use specialist terms correctly.
- Marks will not be deducted for incorrect answers.
- There are no blank pages.

Advice to candidates
- Work steadily through the paper.
- Don't spend too long on one question.
- If you have time at the end, go back and check your answers.

SECTION A

Answer ALL questions.

For each part of question 1, choose an answer A, B, C or D and put a cross in the box. Mark only one answer for each question. If you change your mind about an answer, put a line through the box and then mark your new answer with a cross.

E.g.: Mark the box like this:

☒ A
☒ B
☒ **C**   *This shows your answer*
☒ D

If you change your mind, mark the boxes like this:

☒ **A**   *This shows your final answer*
☒ B
☒ **C**   *First answer*
☒ D

1   (a)   Which of the following roles in sport involves controlling game activity, and making sure that the players obey the rules?

☒ **A** Organiser

☒ **B** Captain

☒ **C** Coach

☒ **D** Official

(1)

(b)   Every training session should be made up of a warm-up, a main activity, and a cool-down.

Why is cooling-down after exercise important?

☒ **A** It increases the amount of lactic acid in muscles.

☒ **B** It increases heart rate.

☒ **C** It prevents muscle stiffness and soreness.

☒ **D** It decreases vital capacity.

(1)

(c) Which of the following is a method of testing cardiovascular endurance?

    ☒ **A** Cooper's twelve-minute run test

    ☒ **B** Hand grip test

    ☒ **C** Sit and reach test

    ☒ **D** Standing broad jump test

(1)

(d) Flexibility is:

    ☒ **A** The ability to change your body's position quickly.

    ☒ **B** The amount of movement possible at a joint.

    ☒ **C** The ability to use two or more parts of your body together.

    ☒ **D** How well a task is completed.

(1)

(e) Which of the following is a long-term benefit of regular exercise?

    ☒ **A** Increased resting heart rate.

    ☒ **B** Increased blood pressure.

    ☒ **C** Increased stroke volume.

    ☒ **D** Increased breathing rate.

(1)

(f) The SMART principle can be used to set goals in physical activity.
What does the M in SMART stand for?

    ☒ **A** Measurable

    ☒ **B** Motivational

    ☒ **C** Manual

    ☒ **D** Mental

(1)

(g) Which of the following sports would an extrovert be most likely to take part in?

  ☒ **A** Archery

  ☒ **B** Orienteering

  ☒ **C** Golf

  ☒ **D** Basketball

(1)

(h) Doing press ups works which of the following muscle groups most?

  ☒ **A** Hamstrings

  ☒ **B** Latissimus dorsi

  ☒ **C** Triceps

  ☒ **D** Quadriceps

(1)

(i) Which principle of training states that any improvement in fitness caused by training will be gradually lost when training is stopped?

  ☒ **A** Reversibility

  ☒ **B** Recovery

  ☒ **C** Overload

  ☒ **D** Relaxation

(1)

(j) The RICE method can be used to treat injuries like strains and sprains. What does the C in RICE stand for?

  ☒ **A** Contraction

  ☒ **B** Compression

  ☒ **C** Circulation

  ☒ **D** Concussion

(1)

(Total 10 marks)

124

SECTION B

Answer ALL questions.

2   Eating a balanced diet is an important part of a healthy lifestyle.

Complete each of the following statements with a nutrient that should be included in a balanced diet:

(a)   .... are made up of molecules called amino acids.
They help the body to grow and to repair itself.

(1)

(b)   .... should be included in the diet as the main source of
energy for the body.

(1)

(Total 2 marks)

3   Regular participation in physical activity can improve your social and mental well-being, as well as your physical fitness.

(a) Give **one** social benefit of taking part in regular physical activity.

....

....

(1)

(b) Give **one** mental benefit of taking part in regular physical activity.

....

....

(1)

(Total 2 marks)

4 To be able to run and kick the ball in football, the leg has to bend at the knee joint. The knee is one example of a hinge joint.

(a) Complete the following statement about hinge joints:

.... and extension are the two types of movement that are possible at a hinge joint.

(1)

(b) During a match, a footballer falls and dislocates his knee. Describe this type of injury.

....

....

(1)

(Total 2 marks)

5 **Figure 1** shows a gymnast performing a routine on the rings.

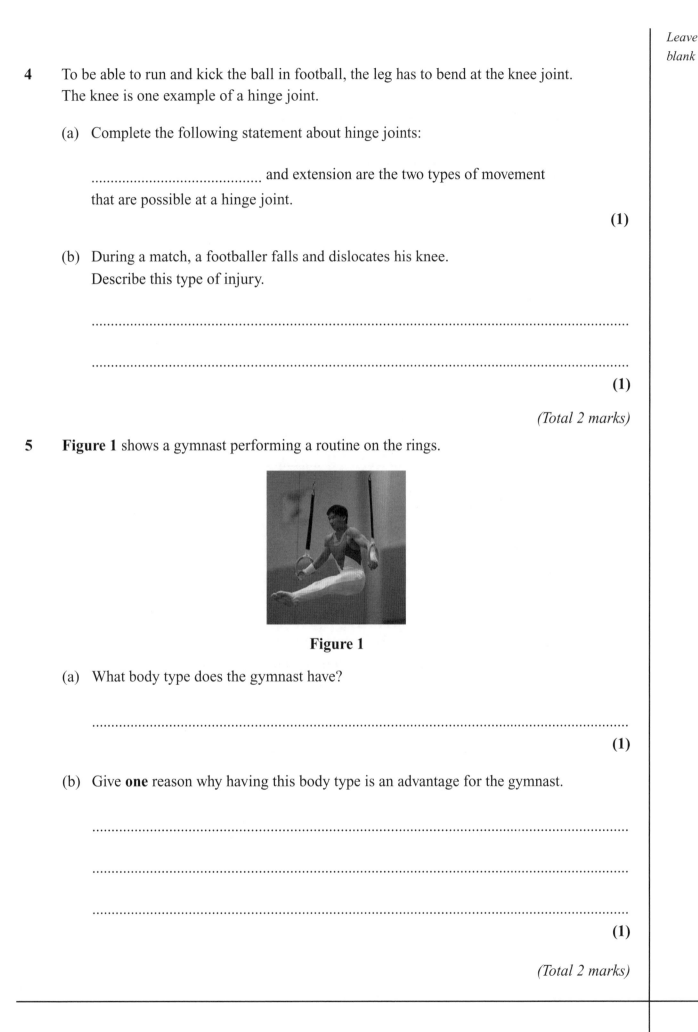

Figure 1

(a) What body type does the gymnast have?

....

(1)

(b) Give **one** reason why having this body type is an advantage for the gymnast.

....

....

....

(1)

(Total 2 marks)

6 The cardiovascular system is responsible for keeping muscles supplied with oxygen.

(a) Identify **one** short-term effect of physical activity on the cardiovascular system.

....

(1)

(b) During vigorous exercise, muscles respire anaerobically, causing an oxygen debt to build up.

(i) Name the acid produced during anaerobic respiration.

....

(1)

(ii) What is meant by the term 'oxygen debt'?

....

....

....

(2)

(Total 4 marks)

7 An athlete's optimum weight depends on the activity that he or she does.
Most sumo wrestlers are obese when at their optimum weight.

(a) What is meant by the term **obese**?

....

(1)

(b) Identify **two** other factors that could affect an athlete's optimum weight.

....

....

(2)

(Total 3 marks)

8 The student shown in **Figure 2** is a good all-round sportsperson, who has joined her school's tennis club. She wants to train, so that she can play for the club in tennis tournaments.

Figure 2

Complete the table below.

(a) Describe **one** example of how each component of fitness is needed when playing tennis.

(3)

(b) Name a test that could be used to monitor each component of fitness during training.

(3)

Component of fitness used	(a) Example	(b) Test
Coordination		
Agility		
Power		

(Total 6 marks)

128

9 There are many different factors that can affect performance.

(a) Explain, using examples, how aggression can affect performance.

....

....

....

....

....

....

....

....

....

....

(4)

(b) The use of steroids is banned in most sports.

(i) Explain why an athlete might risk taking steroids.

....

....

(2)

(ii) Give **one** possible negative side-effect of taking steroids.

....

(1)

(Total 7 marks)

10 Describe how a performer can minimise their risk of injury when taking part
in a physical activity.

....

....

....

....

....

....

....

....

....

(4)

(Total 4 marks)

130

11 Television coverage of sporting events can increase participation, and can also drive the development of technological innovations in sport.

(a) State **two** ways that the media can positively influence **participation** in physical activity.

....

....

....

....

....

(2)

(b) In 2001, broadcasters began to use the 'Hawkeye' system during televised cricket coverage. Briefly describe how 'Hawkeye' is used in cricket matches.

....

....

....

....

....

(2)

(Total 4 marks)

12 The Government works with schools and sports organisations to encourage young people to participate and remain involved in physical activity.

(a) In 2003, the Government set up the PESSCL strategy to improve sports provision in schools. What does PESSCL stand for?

....

....

(1)

(b) Describe, using examples, **two** ways in which Government initiatives encourage young people to have a healthy, active lifestyle.

....

....

....

....

....

....

....

....

(4)

(Total 5 marks)

132

13 Helen is 15, and is taking GCSE PE. She has a resting heart rate of 72 bpm, and wants to improve her fitness.

(a) What does the term 'resting heart rate' mean?

....

....

(1)

(b) Helen wants to do some aerobic training to improve her cardiovascular fitness. To do this she needs to make sure that her heart rate is in the aerobic training zone. Calculate the thresholds of Helen's aerobic training zone.

....

....

....

....

(3)

(c) Helen has to fill out a PAR-Q before she can start training. Explain what a PAR-Q is, and why it should be completed before starting a new activity.

....

....

....

....

(2)

(Total 6 marks)

14 Your location can influence your choice of physical activities, and can also affect how well you perform them.

(a) Explain how where you live may influence the physical activities you choose to do.

....

....

....

....

....

(3)

(b) Explain how different environmental features of the place where you exercise can affect your performance.

....

....

....

....

....

(3)

(Total 6 marks)

15 Matthew plays for his school hockey team.

To improve his performance, Matthew trains by jogging for half an hour twice a week. After a month, he finds that his fitness is no longer improving because he is not achieving overload.

(a) What is meant by **overload**?

....

....

(1)

(b) Using the FITT principle, describe how Matthew could alter his training to achieve overload.

....

....

....

....

....

....

....

....

....

....

(4)

(Total 5 marks)

16 Discuss how someone's gender might affect their participation in physical activity.

(Answer in continuous prose)

....

....

....

....

....

....

....

....

....

....

....

....

....

....

....

....

....

(6)

(Total 6 marks)

17   **Figure 3** shows Roland swimming in a regional competition.

Figure 3

Roland wants to design a personal exercise plan that will help him to improve his competition performances.

Suggest **two** different training methods that Roland could include in his training plan. Explain how each method you suggest would help to improve his performance in swimming, and how it could be adapted to suit Roland's specific needs.

(Answer in continuous prose)

....

....

....

....

....

....

....

....

....

....

....

....

....

....

....

....

....

....

(6)

(Total 6 marks)

END

Practice Exam 2

If you're doing an AQA course, some of your exam questions will be about a pre-released scenario. You'll get a copy of the scenario a few weeks before your exam.

Have a good read of the scenario. Think about what issues it raises, which topics from PE it touches on, and what questions you might be asked about them. It's a good idea to make notes, so scribble on the sheet as much as you like. Make sure that you've revised any topics that you think are relevant to the scenario really thoroughly.

You can't take your own sheet, or your notes, into the exam with you. But you'll get a lovely clean copy of the scenario inside the exam paper, so you don't have to memorise it. There's a copy of the scenario inside our practice paper too (over the page). Use the copy below to read and take notes, and use the second one when you do the paper itself.

(If you're doing a different exam board, it's still worth having a go at this paper — it's still great practice for answering GCSE PE questions.)

General Certificate of Secondary Education

GCSE Physical Education

Pre-Release Material

To be distributed to candidates before the exam.

The examination will be made up of questions that are linked to the scenario below.

> Naomi is 14 years old. She is a skilled football player, and plays for her school team. She trains once a week with the rest of the football team, and has a good level of cardiovascular endurance.
>
> Naomi has recently started her GCSE courses, and is taking GCSE PE. Because she is studying PE, Naomi wants to increase her participation in physical activities. Her local sports centre has a range of activities and classes available, but she is not sure which one she wants to do.
>
> Naomi has also decided that she would like to do some voluntary work. Her PE teacher put Naomi in touch with a local football club, who asked her to help coach their junior football team. She now helps out with their training sessions every Tuesday evening. When she can manage to, Naomi also goes along to watch the team play, and to support them. The junior team is sponsored by a local garden centre.

General Certificate of Secondary Education

GCSE Physical Education

Paper 2

Centre name					
Centre number					
Candidate number					

Time allowed:

45 minutes

Surname	
Other names	
Candidate signature	

Instructions to candidates
- Write your name and other details in the spaces provided above.
- Answer **all** questions in the spaces provided.
- Do all rough work on the paper.

Information for candidates
- The maximum mark available for this paper is **40**.
- The marks available are given in brackets at the end of each question or part-question.
- In questions 1 (c) and 2 (c) your communication skills will be assessed. You should answer these questions in continuous prose and use specialist terms correctly.
- Marks will not be deducted for incorrect answers.
- There are no blank pages.

Advice to candidates
- Work steadily through the paper.
- Don't spend too long on one question.
- If you have time at the end, go back and check your answers.

All of the questions on this exam paper are linked to the scenario that was given to you before the exam. This scenario is copied again below.

Naomi is 14 years old. She is a skilled football player, and plays for her school team. She trains once a week with the rest of the football team, and has a good level of cardiovascular endurance.

Naomi has recently started her GCSE courses, and is taking GCSE PE. Because she is studying PE, Naomi wants to increase her participation in physical activities. Her local sports centre has a range of activities and classes available, but she is not sure which one she wants to do.

Naomi has also decided that she would like to do some voluntary work. Her PE teacher put Naomi in touch with a local football club, who asked her to help coach their junior football team. She now helps out with their training sessions every Tuesday evening. When she can manage to, Naomi also goes along to watch the team play, and to support them. The junior team is sponsored by a local garden centre.

---

1 (a) (i) Explain what is meant by the term 'cardiovascular endurance'.

....

....

(1)

(ii) Suggest why having good cardiovascular endurance can be an advantage when playing football.

....

....

....

(1)

(b) Explain why it is important that Naomi allows herself enough time to rest between her exercise sessions.

....

....

....

....

....

....

....

....

(4)

Question 1 continues on the next page

(c) There are a wide range of activities on offer at Naomi's local sports centre.
Explain, using examples, what factors may affect the physical activities that Naomi
chooses to participate in.

(Answer in continuous prose)

....

....

....

....

....

....

....

....

....

....

....

....

....

....

....

(8)

(Total 14 marks)

2 (a) Describe **two** benefits that Naomi might get from doing voluntary work coaching the team.

....

....

....

....

....

....

(2)

(b) The team that Naomi coaches are taking part in a knock-out football tournament. Briefly outline the structure of a knock-out competition.

....

....

....

....

....

....

(3)

Question 2 continues on the next page

(c) Describe, using examples, how Naomi could give feedback and guidance to the players she coaches. Explain how her feedback could help them to improve their performance.

....

....

....

....

....

....

....

....

....

....

....

....

....

....

....

....

....

(8)

(d) Describe some of the advantages of sponsorship for the junior football team
     and for their sponsors.

....

....

....

....

....

....

....

....

....

....

....

....

....

....

....

(6)

Question 2 continues on the next page

(e) Describe how Naomi could reduce the risk of the children she coaches being injured during training.

(Answer in continuous prose)

....

....

....

....

....

....

....

....

....

....

....

....

....

....

....

....

(7)

(Total 26 marks)

END

Section One — Roles In Sport

Page 7 (Warm-Up Questions)

1) Health is a state of complete mental, physical and social well-being, and not just the absence of disease and infirmity.

2) Competence is the relationship between skill, and knowing how and when to use skills, tactics, strategies and compositional ideas. To be competent you need to be physically and mentally ready to do an activity.

3) P - Personal hygiene, E - Emotional health, A - Alcohol/drug use, S - Safety, E - Environment, D - Diet.

4) Physical activity is just any form of movement. Exercise is physical activity that you do to improve or maintain your health and/or fitness.

5) Any three from: player/performer / organiser / choreographer / official / coach / captain / volunteer.

6) Organisers arrange and coordinate competitions and events, and organise people, facilities and time. Being an organiser can also involve supervising other people, and delegating tasks.

7) To be a good coach, you need to be able to lead and influence a group. You need to be enthusiastic about your sport and able to motivate yourself and your team. To help players and performers improve, you need to be able to set goals and monitor and evaluate performance. You also need to be able to communicate clearly, as well as listen and respond to the players.

8) E.g. by volunteering, people can sustain their participation in sport. They can also increase their knowledge of a sport. They can improve their leadership and teamwork skills, as well as making new friends. They can gain valuable experience, which can make them more employable. They can also make useful contacts within a sport.

Pages 8-9 (Exam Questions)

1 C *(1 mark)*

2 A *(1 mark)*

3 D *(1 mark)*

4 a) Exercise is a physical activity *(1 mark)* done to improve or maintain health and/or fitness *(1 mark)*.

  b) E.g. any two from: being satisfied and happy with life / having more positive feelings than negative ones / having plenty of access to green space / doing a range of activities *(1 mark for each correct answer, maximum 2 marks)*.

5 a) E.g. any three from: increased fitness / improved health / improved performance / making new friends / improved co-operation and teamwork skills / increased happiness / stress relief / increased self-esteem / enjoyment *(1 mark for each correct answer, maximum 3 marks)*.

  b) E.g. any two from: good personal hygiene / avoidance of stress / avoiding misuse of alcohol/drugs / not smoking / using proper safety equipment at work and when playing sport / access to green spaces / having a balanced diet *(1 mark for each correct answer, maximum 2 marks)*.

  c) E.g. blocking opponents shots effectively to prevent them scoring *(1 mark)*.

6 a) Any one of: organiser / official / coach *(1 mark)*.

  b) Organiser — e.g. any three of: she must be good at supervising others / good at delegating tasks to others / good at showing initiative / good attention to detail / organised / good at promoting events.
  Official — e.g. any three of: she needs to know the rules very well / be observant / be decisive/confident so she can keep control of the game / be able to communicate clearly.
  Coach — e.g. any three of: she needs to know the rules very well / be good at adapting her methods to suit individual players / be good at communicating her ideas clearly / good at listening / good at goal setting / good at motivating others to perform / good at performance analysis / good at giving feedback.
  (1 mark for each correct answer, maximum 3 marks)
  This is a three mark question, so you need to give three qualities that match the role you named in part (a).

Section Two — Exercise and the Human Body

Page 15 (Warm-Up Questions)

1) Vital organs.

2) Muscles can only pull.

3) Extension.

4) Tendons, ligaments, and cartilage.

5) E.g. shoulder / hip.

6) Antagonistic muscles.

7) Isotonic contraction.

Page 16 (Exam Questions)

1 A *(1 mark)*

2 a) A — trapezius *(1 mark)*

    B — triceps *(1 mark)*

    C — latissimus dorsi *(1 mark)*

    D — gluteals/gluteus maximus *(1 mark)*

    E — hamstring *(1 mark)*

    F — gastrocnemius *(1 mark)*

  b) E.g. press ups *(1 mark)*.

  c) The quadriceps *(1 mark)*.

Page 20 (Warm-Up Questions)

1) Oxygen.

2) Red blood cells.

3) Glucose.

4) Aerobic respiration.

5) Lactic acid.

6) The volume of air that moves in and out of the lungs when you breathe normally.

7) Arteries.

Page 21 (Exam Questions)

1 D *(1 mark)*

2 a) The most air you could possibly breathe in after breathing out the largest volume of air you can *(1 mark)*.

  b) If you have a large vital capacity, you can take in a large amount of oxygen with each breath *(1 mark)*, so you will be able to keep your muscles supplied with plenty of oxygen as you exercise *(1 mark)*. This means you will be able to keep exercising (aerobically) for long periods of time *(1 mark)*.

3 a) One in which physical activity is done at a slow or steady rate *(1 mark)* and the heart and lungs can supply the muscles with all the oxygen that they need *(1 mark)*.

  b) Glucose + Oxygen *(1 mark)* → Energy + Carbon dioxide + Water *(1 mark)*
  Make sure you know both respiration equations, and don't get them mixed up.

4 a) Anaerobic respiration happens when the muscles need more oxygen than the body can provide *(1 mark)*.

  b) The by-product of anaerobic respiration is lactic acid *(1 mark)*. It gradually builds up, causing fatigue in muscles *(1 mark)*.

Page 25 (Warm-Up Questions)

1) The amount of blood pumped by a ventricle with each contraction.

2) Multiply your heart rate by your stroke volume

3) Breathing rate gets quicker.

4) It gets faster.

5) The force on blood vessel walls caused by blood.

6) Systolic blood pressure is the pressure when the left ventricle contracts, diastolic is the pressure when the left ventricle is relaxed.

7) To increase blood flow to the muscles, and to cool the body (by moving blood closer to the surface of the skin). This process is called blood shunting / vascular shunting.

Page 26 (Exam Questions)

1 C *(1 mark)*

2 Rest gives time for your muscles to adapt *(1 mark)* and recover *(1 mark)*. If you don't rest for long enough, you risk getting injured *(1 mark)*.

3 a) Weight-bearing exercises increase bone density *(1 mark)* and strengthens bones *(1 mark)*.

  b) E.g. any two from: walking / running / tennis / aerobics.
  (1 mark for each weight-bearing exercise, maximum 2 marks)

4 a) Your respiratory muscles get stronger *(1 mark)*, so they can make your chest cavity larger *(1 mark)*, giving you a greater vital capacity *(1 mark)*.

   b) To keep taking in high amounts of oxygen in order to repay the oxygen debt *(1 mark)*, and to remove waste products such as lactic acid *(1 mark)*.

Section Three — Health and Fitness

Page 34 (Warm-Up Questions)

1) Health-related fitness means you can do everyday activities without feeling too tired. Skill-related fitness is the fitness required to play a sport to a high level.

2) Body composition is the percentage of body weight made up by fat, muscle and bone.

3) It gives an idea of whether a person is a healthy weight or not.

4) A sprinter leaving the starting blocks.

5) The time it takes you to move in response to something.

6) Strength and speed.

7) E.g. you need to know how to pace yourself, and know when to start sprinting for the finish.

Page 35 (Exam Questions)

1 B *(1 mark)*

2 D *(1 mark)*

3 Muscular endurance is the ability to repeatedly use your voluntary muscles over a long time without getting tired *(1 mark)*. E.g. a runner with good muscular endurance will be able to run for a long time without getting tired *(1 mark)*.

4 E.g. being fit is part of having physical well-being *(1 mark)*, but to be healthy you need social and mental well-being too *(1 mark)*. / You can have high levels of physical fitness, but have an unhealthy lifestyle, e.g. taking drugs, eating an unbalanced diet *(2 marks)*.

5 a) Muscular strength is the amount of force a muscle can apply *(1 mark)*.

   b) Any two from: e.g. a good level of muscular strength can mean you can do everyday activities (e.g. carrying a child) without getting too tired / without getting injured / it enables you to participate in physical activity / it gives you a wider choice of activities you can participate in.
   (1 mark for each valid reason, up to a maximum of 2 marks)
   There are two marks available, so try to come up with two ways that muscular strength can help you to have a healthy, active lifestyle.

6 E.g.

Sport	a) Fitness Component	b) Example of use
Rugby	Strength	**To push in scrum/hand-off**
Tennis	**Power**	To serve and smash
Sprinting	**Speed**	To win the race
Gymnastics	Flexibility	**To get into different positions**

   (1 mark for each correct fitness component. 1 mark for each example of component use relevant to the activity.)

7 a) The ability to control the movement of your entire body *(1 mark)*, and to be able to change your body's position quickly *(1 mark)*.

   b) For example, football needs agility to turn quickly *(1 mark)*, balance so you don't fall over *(1 mark)* and coordination so you make contact with the ball *(1 mark)*.
   (1 mark each for a suitable point for each component).

8 E.g. A squash player needs to have good coordination *(1 mark)* so that they can hit the ball correctly with the racquet *(1 mark)*. They also need to have good agility *(1 mark)* to change direction on the court quickly *(1 mark)*.
   (1 mark for each relevant component of fitness, 1 mark for how it would be useful to a squash player. Maximum of 4 marks.)

Page 43 (Warm-Up Questions)

1) E.g. Strength, cardiovascular fitness, flexibility.

2) Some disabilities can make particular activities harder to do, and so can negatively affect performance.

3) Body shape.

4) Endomorph, mesomorph and ectomorph.

5) Age, gender, muscle girth, activity, bone structure.

6) Weighing less than is normal, needed or healthy.

7) Anorexia is an eating disorder where suffers starve themselves because they believe they're fat.

Page 44 (Exam Questions)

1 C *(1 mark)*

2 Any three from: e.g. in general men have larger physiques / better metabolisms / more muscle / in general women have less muscle / are more flexible / women physically mature earlier.
   (Any 3 physical factors, maximum 3 marks)

3 a) A person's expected weight is the weight you would expect them to be based on their height *(1 mark)*. A person's optimum weight is the weight at which they perform best in their chosen sport *(1 mark)*.

   b) E.g. he will be able to pin his opponents more effectively / it will be harder for his opponents to move/throw him *(1 mark)*.

4 E.g. Playing football requires high levels of strength and endurance. These aspects of fitness decline as you get older, so footballers tend to be fairly young. Playing golf does not require high levels of strength and endurance, so older people are not disadvantaged. Older players will also have more experience which will increase their levels of performance.
   (1 mark for each sensible reason, maximum of 4 marks)

Page 49 (Warm-Up Questions)

1) A diet that contains the best ratio of nutrients to match your lifestyle.

2) Having too much LDL cholesterol increases the risk of heart attacks and strokes. High levels of HDL cholesterol help the body get rid of excess cholesterol.

3) Tar in cigarette smoke clogs up the alveoli making it harder for gas exchange to take place.

4) It increases it.

5) To improve performance.

6) Tobacco and alcohol.

7) Any three from: e.g. beta blockers / anabolic steroids / diuretics / stimulants / narcotic analgesics / peptide hormones.

Page 50 (Exam Questions)

1 C *(1 mark)*

2 Chris may eat more protein *(1 mark)* in order to build up his muscles *(1 mark)*. Val may eat more carbohydrates *(1 mark)* before a race to provide her with the energy that she requires *(1 mark)*.

3 a) E.g.

Name of Drug	Reason drug is taken	Side Effects
Stimulants	**speed up reactions**	high blood pressure
Narcotic Analgesics	kill pain so an athlete can train for longer/harder	constipation
EPO / Peptide hormones	**increases red blood cell production (and so cardiovascular endurance)**	abnormal growth
Diuretics	weight loss caused by frequent urination	**cramp**
Beta blockers	**reduce anxiety**	addiction

   (1 mark for each correct entry)
   There are loads of different reasons and effects you could have written in this table, but remember to get the marks, you only really need one effect and one side effect for each drug.

   b) Blood doping is where an athlete injects blood/EPO *(1 mark)* to increase the number of red blood cells in their blood stream *(1 mark)*. This increases the oxygen supply to their muscles *(1 mark)* which can improve their performance in an aerobic activity *(1 mark)*.

Section Four — Training and Sporting Skills

Page 57 (Warm-Up Questions)

1) You might not have the strength or endurance for high intensity sports, and you might permanently injure yourself by doing them.

2) Physical Activity Readiness Questionnaire

3) Any two of: e.g. measuring blood pressure / checking lifestyle and family history / measuring body mass index (BMI) / measuring resting heart rate.

4) Any three of: e.g. Cooper's 12-minute run test / treadmill test / multi-stage fitness test / Harvard step test.

5) Calliper test: pinch the skin and the underlying fat using skin fold callipers. Record this measurement. It can be used to estimate your body fat percentage. Body density test: weigh yourself on land, and underwater. These two measurements can be used to calculate body density, and body fat percentage.

6) E.g. 50 m sprint test / 30 m sprint test.

7) E.g. because it only takes weight and height into account. You could be healthy and just have a large amount of muscle, but your BMI may show you're at an unhealthy weight.

Page 58 (Exam Questions)

1 C *(1 mark)*

2 D *(1 mark)*

3 a) Any two of: balance / flexibility / muscular strength / agility / coordination *(1 mark for each component, maximum 2 marks)*.

   b) *For example:*
   Balance — the standing stork test *(1 mark)*. Stand on one leg with your other foot touching your knee, your hands on your hips, and the heel of the foot you are standing on off the floor *(1 mark)*. Time how long you can stand like that without moving your feet or your hands *(1 mark)*.
   Remember to say what measurement is being recorded, as well as what the person being tested needs to do.

4 *For example:*
   The sit and reach test (for flexibility). The student should sit on the floor with their legs straight out in front of them. Then they push a ruler, placed on a box, as far forwards as they can with their fingers (keeping their legs straight). The distance that they can push the ruler is a measure of their flexibility.
   The ruler drop test (for reactions). The tester holds a ruler vertically, with the 0 cm mark in line with the top of the student's thumb. The tester drops the ruler, and the student must try to catch it. The distance that the ruler falls before the student catches it is a measure of their reactions.

   (1 mark for each named test of flexibility, reactions or muscular endurance. Up to 2 marks for each test description)

Page 61 (Warm-Up Questions)

1) Cool-down

2) Specificity, progression, overload, reversibility (or rest and recovery), tedium

3) A Personal Exercise Programme.

4) To give your muscles the chance to adapt, and to repair the damage caused by physical activity.

5) Both

Page 62 (Exam Questions)

1 a) It is likely to have decreased *(1 mark)*.

   b) Athletes need to leave enough time to rest and recover after exercise (especially after an injury) *(1 mark)*, but not too much so that their fitness level drops *(1 mark)*.

2 a) Janice could include different activities in her training sessions (such as cycling or swimming) so that she doesn't get so bored *(1 mark)*. She could gradually increase the amount of time that she trains for / the frequency of her training sessions / the intensity of her training to make sure she achieves overload *(1 mark)*.
   There are two marks available, so try to come up with two suggestions.

   b) Any one of: e.g. a cool-down pays off oxygen debt / gets rid of lactic acid in the muscles / prevents muscle soreness/stiffness *(1 mark)*.

3 Progression *(1 mark)* — steadily increasing the amount of training *(1 mark)*.
   Overload *(1 mark)* — making your body work hard enough to make it fitter *(1 mark)*.

Either: Reversibility *(1 mark)* — any improvement in fitness through training will gradually reverse and be lost when you stop training *(1 mark)*.
Or: Rest and recovery *(1 mark)* — you should allow enough rest time in your training programme for your body to repair any damage caused by physical activity *(1 mark)*.
Tedium *(1 mark)* — training should be interesting as well as useful to prevent boredom *(1 mark)*.
Remember the SPORT principles of training.

Page 71 (Warm-Up Questions)

1) A rep is one single complete movement, a set is the number of reps you do before having a rest.

2) E.g. it improves overall fitness / more interesting than other methods / easily adapted to a person's needs.

3) In an eccentric muscle contraction, a muscle gets stretched and lengthens.

4) Static, dynamic, PNF

5) E.g. weight training and plyometric training.

6) Strength, flexibility and cardiovascular endurance.

7) pre-season preparation, competition/peak season, closed-season

8) The difference between your maximum and resting heart rates.

Pages 72-73 (Exam Questions)

1 C *(1 mark)*

2 A *(1 mark)*

3 E.g. weight training *(1 mark)* — an anaerobic training method *(1 mark)*

4 a) E.g. Continuous training *(1 mark)*, as it has no rest periods and is most like cross-country / it is an aerobic activity *(1 mark)*.
   Interval training or Fartlek training would also be okay here.

   b) E.g. Continuous training can be really boring *(1 mark)*.

   c) Any one of: e.g. George could make each of his training sessions longer/ train for forty minutes rather than thirty / George could increase the intensity of his training sessions/go running rather than jogging *(1 mark for any sensible suggestion)*.

5 a) Any one of: Circuit training / fartlek training / interval training / cross-training *(1 mark)*

   b) Any one of, e.g.: it will not improve Fiona's sprinting / anaerobic fitness / agility / strength / power / coordination / reaction times (all of which she will need to play hockey well) *(1 mark)*.

6 Paddy is fitter. The graph shows that Dee's heart rate goes up higher *(1 mark)* and quicker *(1 mark)* than Paddy's. Paddy's resting heart rate is lower *(1 mark)*. Paddy's heart rate returns to pre-exercise levels much quicker *(1 mark)*.
   This is a big four mark question, so you need to go into plenty of detail about what the graph tells you about the students' fitness.

7 At higher altitudes the air pressure is lower — which means you take in less oxygen with each breath as you exercise *(1 mark)*. The body makes more red blood cells so enough oxygen can still be supplied to the body *(1 mark)*. Athletes train at high altitude to increase their red blood cell count, then compete at low altitude while they still have some of these extra red blood cells *(1 mark)*. This means they have a much better oxygen supply to their muscles *(1 mark)*, which increases their ability to do aerobic activity.

Page 78 (Warm-Up Questions)

1) pre-determined, efficient, coordinated, fluent, aesthetic

2) open

3) E.g. whether the bowler has bowled a wide ball.

4) E.g. breaking a tennis serve into the ball toss and racquet motion and practising them separately.

5) You can improve a skill by increasing the range, difficulty, consistency, precision, control, or fluency of the skill.

6) When you can feel how well you've done a technique.

Page 79 (Exam Questions)

1 B *(1 mark)*

2 A *(1 mark)*

3 a) A skill is a learned ability *(1 mark)* to bring about the result you want, with maximum certainty and efficiency *(1 mark)*.

b) It's a mixture of both *(1 mark)*. Taking a football penalty can be defined as a closed skill because it is not greatly affected by factors such as the wind *(1 mark)*. However, it can also be defined as an open skill because you can change the speed and aim of the shot in response to the goalkeeper's position or movement *(1 mark)*.

4 Whole practice — practising a whole technique in one go *(1 mark)*.
Part practice — breaking up a technique into parts and practising them separately *(1 mark)*.
Fixed practice — repeatedly practising doing a technique in one situation *(1 mark)*.
Variable practice — repeating the technique in many situations *(1 mark)*.

Page 84 (Warm-Up Questions)

1) An extrovert.

2) E.g. it can improve performance by increasing confidence and helping you to deal with stress.

3) E.g. prize money

4) Specific, measurable, achievable, realistic, time-bound

5) So you can know when you've achieved your goal.

6) E.g. good feedback can help you to focus on what you want to improve.

7) E.g. to reduce the risk of getting injured.

Page 85 (Exam Questions)

1 C *(1 mark)*

2 Intrinsic motivation comes from inside you *(1 mark)*, e.g. you might coach a team because you enjoy it *(1 mark)*. Extrinsic motivation comes from outside *(1 mark)*, e.g. a coach may get paid *(1 mark)*.
Don't just explain what extrinsic and intrinsic motivation are — you need to give examples of both for a coach to get all the marks.

3 a) Either: Anxiety can increase a performer's skill level *(1 mark)* by increasing their arousal level / awareness *(1 mark)*.
Or: If a performer gets too anxious, their nerves may prevent them from performing a skill to the best of their ability *(1 mark)*, so their skill level will decrease *(1 mark)*.

b) Motivation can increase a performer's skill level *(1 mark)* by increasing their arousal level / increasing their desire to win / decreasing their arousal levels (if their stress levels are too high) *(1 mark)*.

4 E.g. goal setting can help an athlete to focus on what they want to achieve. Setting goals can help to motivate a performer. Goal setting helps to ensure exercise adherence / helps an athlete to stick to their training programme. Setting short term, achievable goals can help an athlete to feel in control, and reduce their anxiety. Reaching a goal can boost confidence (and give a sense of achievement).
(1 mark for each sensible point, up to a maximum of 4 marks.)

Page 89 (Warm-Up Questions)

1) Get a first aider / give them appropriate first aid / ring for an ambulance if necessary.

2) E.g. cuts and bruises.

3) When tissues swell and become sore.

4) E.g. tennis elbow / golfer's elbow / tendonitis / shin splints.

5) Rest, Ice, Compression and Elevation.

6) An open fracture is when the skin is broken by the bone. A closed fracture is one where the skin is intact.

7) Stop exercising, take deep breaths, breathe out slowly.

Page 90 (Exam Questions)

1 B *(1 mark)*

2 a) A break in a bone *(1 mark)*.

b) A compound fracture is a complete break in the bone *(1 mark)*, where the bone sticks out of the skin *(1 mark)*. A greenstick fracture is a closed fracture (the skin isn't broken) *(1 mark)* where the bone is only partially broken *(1 mark)*.

3 a) Hypothermia *(1 mark)*.
Any two of, e.g: rigid muscles / irregular heartbeat / unconsciousness
(1 mark for each correct symptom, maximum 2 marks).

b) E.g. Rosie needs to steadily raise the body temperature of the sufferer to 37 °C *(1 mark)*. She could give extra clothing or a blanket / sleeping bag

to the sufferer *(1 mark)*. She could also give them a hot drink *(1 mark)*.
Part b) is worth three marks — so make sure that your answer mentions three different ways to treat the condition.

4 Symptoms — Unconsciousness *(1 mark)*, disorientation *(1 mark)* and memory loss *(1 mark)*. If unconscious, place the person in the recovery position and get an ambulance *(1 mark)*. If they're conscious, keep the person under observation for 24 hours *(1 mark)*.

Section Five — Sport in Society

Page 99 (Warm-Up Questions)

1) Leisure is free time you can use to do whatever you want.

2) E.g. less time is spent working, technology has made doing chores like cleaning quicker.

3) Recreation is something you do in your leisure time to relax or be active, e.g. jogging.

4) E.g. mothers, OAPs

5) Any seven from: e.g. politics, acceptability, challenge, money, lifestyle, skill, status, age, role models, peer pressure, family, gender, race, disability, health.

6) Good teachers can encourage you to exercise, raising your confidence and making it enjoyable. They can also be responsible for the range of activities you have the opportunity to take part in. However a bad PE teacher can put you off doing exercise.

7) E.g. Regularly doing an activity, taking part in sporting events, deciding to become an official and working towards an accreditation.

Page 100 (Exam Questions)

1 D *(1 mark)*

2 Sport is competitive / has rules / competitions / the aim is to win *(1 mark)*. Physical recreation isn't competitive / you can set your own targets *(1 mark)*.

3 a) E.g. John might have a lot of leisure time because he has taken early retirement *(1 mark)*.

b) E.g. John's age could mean that he wants to do less strenuous activities *(1 mark)*.

c) Any two from: e.g.
Money — John may not be able to afford to participate in a more expensive sport e.g. skiing, but can afford to play relatively cheap sports like badminton.
Facilities — John may have easy access to badminton courts. If there were no badminton courts available or the facilities available were poor, John would be unable/less likely to play.
Fashion — Badminton may be fashionable at the moment, which may mean more money is put into providing badminton facilities, giving John more opportunity to play this sport.
Danger — John may dislike more dangerous or high contact sports such as rugby, and so has opted to play badminton because it is a low risk sport.
(2 marks for each well described factor, up to a maximum of 4 marks.)
This is a four mark question, but it's only asking for two things. This should set the alarm bells ringing — you're gonna need to explain each of those two points in order to get all the marks. The word 'discuss' should also give you a clue...

4 *For example*:
Weather — When running the weather can affect your performance, e.g. if it's hot and humid, you'll overheat more quickly and so won't perform as well / you could be running in the same direction as the wind, which would help improve your performance.
Altitude — Running at higher altitudes than normal will negatively affect your performance (as you breathe in less oxygen and so will get tired more quickly).
Terrain — running on a hilly/rough terrain instead of a flat/smooth one will take longer and so negatively affect your performance.
(1 mark for each sensible factor, up to three marks)

Page 108 (Warm-Up Questions)

1) E.g. Top links Programme, Young Ambassadors programme, Gifted and Talented programme, Step into Sport.

2) Healthy eating, physical activity and emotional health and well-being.

3) PE, School Sport and Club Links

4) Elite, Performance, Participation and Foundation

5) League

6) An amateur does not get paid and a professional does.

7) E.g. PE teacher, a sports manager, a sports physiotherapist.

8) A bit of both.

9) E.g. a beer company sponsoring a youth event.

Page 109 (Exam Questions)

1 A *(1 mark)*

2 a) Stage 4 *(1 mark)*

   b) Performers at this level have achieved a level of excellence / will be competing in national and international competitions *(1 mark)*.

3 Start — Increase participation in sport in order to improve the health of the nation (with a focus on priority groups) *(1 mark)*.
Stay — Keep people in sport through an effective network of clubs, sports facilities, coaches, volunteers and competitive opportunities *(1 mark)*.
Succeed — Create opportunities for talented performers to achieve success *(1 mark)*.

4 E.g. Chris could get a scholarship at a college. / He could compete professionally, but put his prize money into a trust fund. / He could get sponsored by a company. / He could accept large expenses payments, or gifts for competing. / He could find a company willing to give him a "token job" that would allow him to train full-time. / He could accept payments and keep quiet about it (though this is illegal). *(1 mark per suggestion, up to a maximum of 3)*
   Although it doesn't tell you to give a certain number of suggestions, you can tell from the marks available that you should write about three ways that Chris could get money to train full-time.

Page 115 (Warm-Up Questions)

1) False

2) E.g. PE is compulsory in both countries.

3) British Olympic Association

4) Games are very expensive to host / threat of terrorism and hooligans / strain on local infrastructure.

5) The director could bias the programme, e.g. by only showing a negative reaction to a referee's decision.

6) If a sport or clothing for a sport is in fashion, people are more likely to do it because it seems cool, and there may be more opportunities to do it.

Page 116 (Exam Questions)

1 D *(1 mark)*

2 a) Any one of: e.g. runs the Olympics / decides where to hold the Games / decides which sports to include / helps to plan the games / fights against doping and corruption *(1 mark)*.

   b) Any two of: e.g. hosting the games gains the city prestige / attracts tourism / attracts trade / the facilities built for the Games can be used afterwards / local businesses get extra trade / organisers can make a profit *(1 mark)*.

   c) E.g. good performances in an Olympic event creates role models *(1 mark)* to inspire people to take up the sport *(1 mark)*.

3 a) E.g. radio / internet / newspapers / magazines.
   (1 mark each for any three of the above)

   b) E.g. people are watching the team on the TV rather than attending games *(1 mark)*, so ticket sales are decreasing / merchandise is not being sold at the ground *(1 mark)*.

EXAM ANSWERS

Paper 1

1 (a) D *(1 mark)*

  (b) C *(1 mark)*

  (c) A *(1 mark)*

  (d) B *(1 mark)*

  (e) C *(1 mark)*

  (f) A *(1 mark)*

  (g) D *(1 mark)*

  (h) C *(1 mark)*

  (i) A *(1 mark)*

  (j) B *(1 mark)*

2 (a) Proteins *(1 mark)*

  (b) Carbohydrates *(1 mark)*

3 (a) E.g. any one of: making new friends / spending time with your friends / learning cooperation / learning to work with other people *(1 mark)*.

  (b) E.g. any one of: relieves stress / improves self-esteem / increases confidence / provides competition / improves your response to pressure / makes you feel good *(1 mark)*.

4 (a) Flexion *(1 mark)*

  (b) Dislocation is when a bone is pulled out of its normal position *(1 mark)*.

5 (a) Mesomorph *(1 mark)*

  (b) E.g. having strong, muscular arms allows the gymnast to lift/support his body weight easily *(1 mark for any sensible reason)*

6 (a) E.g. any one of: increased heart rate / heart muscle contracts more strongly / blood supply to muscles increases (cardiac output) / blood pressure increases *(1 mark)*.

  (b) (i) Lactic acid *(1 mark)*

     (ii) Oxygen debt is the amount of oxygen that you need during recovery / after exercise *(1 mark)* to make up for a shortfall of oxygen during exercise / to break down the lactic acid that has built up in your muscles *(1 mark)*.
     You don't need to use these exact words — as long as you've made it clear that it's the extra amount of oxygen you need after you've been exercising, you get both marks.

7 (a) Obese means very overfat / having a large amount of excess body fat *(1 mark)*.

  (b) Any two of: bone structure / muscle girth / gender / age *(1 mark each for any two valid factors)*.
     There's no mark for saying 'the activity that they do', because you were told that in the question.

8 (a) Coordination — e.g. playing a shot while you are moving / using hand-eye coordination to move your racket and hit the ball *(1 mark for any valid example)*.
     Agility — e.g. changing direction when running around the court to reach the ball *(1 mark for any valid example)*.
     Power — e.g. to serve / smash the ball *(1 mark for any valid example)*.

  (b) Coordination — 3-ball juggle / alternate hand throw *(1 mark)*.
     Agility — Illinois agility run test *(1 mark)*.
     Power — standing broad jump test / vertical jump test / sargent jump test *(1 mark)*.

9 (a) E.g. Aggression can improve your performance because it can help to motivate you / raise your arousal level *(1 mark)*. For example, it may make a swimmer or athlete more determined to win a race / help a tennis player to hit the ball harder *(1 mark)*. It can also make your performance worse if your arousal level is too high / your aggression is not kept under control *(1 mark)*. This may make an athlete more likely to cheat, for example a footballer may lose their temper and deliberately injure an opponent *(1 mark)*.

  (b) (i) Steroids increase bone and muscle growth *(1 mark)*, so they make you stronger, which could improve your performance *(1 mark)*.

     (ii) E.g. any one of: may cause high blood pressure / heart disease / infertility / cancer / uncontrollable aggression / male characteristics in female athletes *(1 mark)*.

10 Performers can minimise their risk of injury by:
   • Assessing their personal readiness before taking up a new activity.
   • Warming-up thoroughly before starting the activity.
   • Using the right equipment for the activity.
   • Using the correct techniques when lifting and carrying equipment.
   • Checking that their own equipment is in good condition.
   • Playing against opponents of the same size, strength, and skill level.
   • Following the rules of the activity.
   • Using the correct technique for the game (e.g. tackling safely).
   • Wearing suitable clothing / footwear.
   • Not wearing jewellery / watches / anything that could get caught.
   • Using any necessary protective clothing or equipment.
   • Cooling-down properly after finishing the activity.
   • Allowing enough time for rest and recovery before playing again.
   (1 mark each for any four valid points.)

11 (a) The media can have a positive effect on participation in physical activity by:
   • Bringing a sport to people who would not have experienced it otherwise, inspiring them to participate in that sport.
   • Producing role models, who might encourage people to participate in their sport.

- Running direct promotional campaigns that encourage people to take/ up a particular sport / increase their participation in physical activity (as part of a healthy, active lifestyle).
  (1 mark each for any two valid points)

(b) A set of cameras is used to track / predict the path of the cricket ball as it is bowled *(1 mark)*. This allows an official to judge whether a batsman is out lbw / the commentators and viewers to assess whether or not the umpire's lbw decisions are correct *(1 mark)*.

12 (a) PE, School Sport and Club Links *(1 mark)*

(b) • Encouraging young people to participate in regular physical activity, e.g. the 'five hour offer' / 5 × 60 initiative, which aims to encourage young people to take part in five hours of physical activity every week.
- Promoting healthy eating in schools, e.g. the Whole School Food Policy, which aims to involve parents, staff and students in planning healthy meals.
- Improving emotional well-being, e.g. as part of the Healthy Schools Policy, all schools must have an anti-bullying policy.
- Encouraging young people to sustain their involvement in physical activity, e.g. through the Step into Sport programme, which encourages young people to train as sports leaders/volunteers.
  (1 mark each for two ways in which the Government promotes healthy, active lifestyles, and 1 mark each for two examples of initiatives.)
  The examples of initiatives given here aren't the only ones you could use — as long as you name one that backs up your point, that's fine. Have a peek back at pages 101-103 for a reminder of all the different initiatives and what they do.

13 (a) Resting heart rate is the number of times the heart beats per minute when a person is at rest *(1 mark)*.

(b) Helen's maximum heart rate = 220 – age = 220 – 15 = 205 bpm *(1 mark)*
Lower threshold of aerobic training zone = 60% of maximum heart rate = 0.6 × 205 = 123 bpm *(1 mark)*
Upper threshold of aerobic training zone = 80% of maximum heart rate = 0.8 × 205 = 164 bpm *(1 mark)*

(c) A PAR-Q is a physical activity readiness questionnaire *(1 mark)*. You should complete a PAR-Q before starting a new activity to make sure that it is safe for you to increase your physical activity *(1 mark)*.

14 (a) • Your choice of physical activities may be limited by the facilities that are available in your area, since you won't be able to take part in an activity regularly if facilities are not available locally.
- You are more likely to use a sports facility if it is easy to get to, so availability of public transport may also affect your choice of activity.
- The environment/terrain in the area where you live may affect your choice of activity. If you live in a rural area, it is more likely that you will be able to do outdoor activities.
- The weather in your local area may affect your choice of physical activity. If it's generally cold and wet, you may be more likely to choose indoor activities.
  (3 marks for any three sensible points)

(b) • If the weather/climate is hot and humid, you'll overheat faster, and won't be able to perform as well.
- If you're exercising at high altitude, you breathe in less oxygen, so you'll get tired more quickly.
- The terrain can affect your performance, e.g. running a set distance on a hilly route will take longer than running the same distance on the flat.
  (3 marks for any three sensible points)

15 (a) Overload is when you make your body work harder than it normally would (during exercise) *(1 mark)*.

(b) • Matthew can increase the frequency of his training sessions e.g. by going jogging three or four times a week.
- Matthew can increase the intensity of his training sessions e.g. he could go running (rather than jogging).
- Matthew can increase the time that he spends on each training session e.g. he could make each training session forty-five minutes long.
- Matthew can vary the type of exercise that he does during his training sessions e.g. he could go swimming sometimes instead.
  (1 mark for each point, up to a maximum of 4 marks.)

16 Your answer should include some of the following points:
- Women are still less likely to participate in activities that have traditionally been regarded as 'male only', like rugby. They may have less opportunity to participate in these activities / be persuaded to take part in traditionally 'female' sports by the attitudes of their peer group/families/society.
- Men may be less likely to participate in activities that have traditionally been regarded as 'female only', like dance or aerobics. They may have less opportunity to participate in these activities / be persuaded to take part in traditionally 'male' sports by the attitudes of their peer group/society.

- There may be locally run 'women only' sessions at facilities like swimming pools and gyms, which may encourage women to participate in physical activity when they otherwise wouldn't.
- There is generally less sponsorship available for women in sport, which means they might be less likely to participate in sport (since they may not be able to afford to participate).
- Because women's sport has a lower media profile than men's sport, there tend to be fewer female sporting role models to inspire women to participate.
- There are generally not as many opportunities for women to sustain their involvement in physical activity as managers, players or officials. So they are less likely to participate in physical activities in this way than men.
- People may be discriminated against because of their gender, and so have less opportunity/motivation to participate in physical activity.

This is a level marked question — the number of marks you get will depend on what points you made, and how well you explained and organised them. The maximum mark for this question is 6 marks.
You get 2 marks for making two brief points.
You get 4 marks for making at least three points that are relevant, and some of which are developed.
You get 6 marks for a well written and organised answer, making at least three points, each of which is relevant and well developed.

17 Training methods that Roland could use include:
- Weight training: Roland could use weight training to improve his muscular strength. This will make his swimming stroke stronger, and help him to move through the water faster. Weight training also improves muscular endurance, which will allow him to use his arms and leg muscles for longer without getting tired. Roland could focus his weight training on the muscles and movements that are most important to his swimming stroke. For example, he might focus his training on his upper arm muscles, or do his swimming stroke on land while holding weights.
- Continuous training: Continuous training improves cardiovascular endurance and muscular endurance. Improving these components of fitness would help Roland to swim for longer without getting tired. He could adapt this method of training to suit his needs by, e.g. swimming at a constant rate for long distances, or by doing any form of aerobic activity (like jogging) that will keep his heart at between 60% and 80% of its maximum rate (ensuring that he achieves overload).
- Circuit training: Roland could set up a circuit with stations designed to improve different aspects of his swimming performance. For example, at one station he could lift weights with his arms, to strengthen his arm muscles and make his stroke stronger. At another he could lift weights with his legs to strengthen his leg muscles, and therefore his kick. At a third station, Roland could run on the spot, to improve his cardiovascular endurance, and a fourth could be stretches to improve his flexibility, which will help to make his swimming stroke more efficient (e.g. his breaststroke kick will become larger and stronger, moving him through the water faster).
- Cross training: Roland can use cross training to improve his overall fitness. He should choose aerobic exercises that do not work the same muscle groups as swimming. For example, he could go cycling or play tennis. Both of these activities will improve his cardiovascular fitness, enabling him to swim for longer without getting tired. He will also allow the muscles that he usually works during swimming to recover, reducing his chances of getting injured.
- Plyometric training: Roland can use plyometric training to improve the power of his muscle movements. This will help to improve his starts and turns, as he jumps off the blocks or pushes off the wall, which will improve his race times. It will also improve the power of his stroke, which will help him to accelerate in the water. Roland should focus his plyometric training on his leg and arm muscles. For example he could do exercises like medicine ball chest passes to increase his arm muscle power, and squat jumps to improve his leg muscle power.
- Interval training: Interval training is an excellent way of improving cardiovascular fitness. Increasing his cardiovascular fitness will help Roland to swim for long periods of time without feeling tired. To do interval training, Roland could alternate sprint swimming a couple of lengths with resting (or treading water) for a fixed amount of time.
- Flexibility training: Increasing his flexibility will make Roland's swimming stroke more efficient (e.g. his breaststroke kick will become larger and stronger, moving him through the water faster). So he will use less energy, and be able to swim at higher speeds for longer. Roland can put together a training session made up of stretches designed to increase his flexibility, including plenty of different arm stretches and leg stretches.

This is a level marked question — the number of marks you get will depend on what points you made, <u>and</u> how well you explained and organised them. The maximum mark for this question is 6 marks.
You get 2 marks for naming an appropriate training method, and briefly explaining an advantage of using that training method.
You get 4 marks for naming two appropriate training methods, and saying for each method <u>either</u> how it could be adapted to suit Roland, <u>or</u> how using it would improve his performance. You could also get 4 marks by naming two appropriate training methods, explaining how one of them could be adapted to suit Roland, <u>and</u> saying how using it would improve his performance.
You get 6 marks for a well written and organised answer, giving two appropriate training methods, explaining how Roland could adapt each to suit his needs, and saying how using them would improve his performance.

Paper 2

1 (a) (i) Cardiovascular endurance is the ability to exercise your whole body for long periods of time / the ability of the heart and lungs to supply oxygen to the muscles over a period of time *(1 mark)*.

  (ii) E.g. players may need to run around the pitch for long periods of time. Someone with good cardiovascular endurance will be able to do this without getting tired *(1 mark)*.

 (b) It is important for Naomi to rest between her exercise sessions because, e.g. rest gives her body time recover (repair any damage caused by training) / resting gives her muscles time to adapt / allowing enough time to rest reduces her risk of injury / rest reduces fatigue / resting helps to prevent muscle soreness and stiffness / rest gives her body time to get rid of any lactic acid that has built up in her muscles.
 (1 mark each for any four valid points)

 (c) Factors which may influence Naomi's choice of activities could include:
  • What facilities the sports centre has available, e.g. if they have a good swimming pool Naomi might take up swimming.
  • The cost of the different activities, e.g. if it costs more for Naomi to go swimming than it does for her to join an aerobics class, she may be more likely to take up aerobics.
  • Her family's attitudes, e.g. if her parents play a certain sport, like tennis, they may encourage Naomi to take it up.
  • The attitudes of her peer group, e.g. if all Naomi's friends like playing basketball, and don't like badminton, Naomi is more likely to choose to take part in basketball than badminton.
  • Naomi's sporting role models, e.g. if one of Naomi's sporting role models is a gymnast, it might make her more likely to try gymnastics.
  • Naomi's gender, e.g. Naomi might be less likely to choose an activity that is traditionally 'male', like boxing. If the sports centre runs women-only classes in certain activities, Naomi might be more likely to choose to go to those, as she may feel more comfortable in them.
  • Naomi's age, e.g. as she is only 14 she shouldn't take part in activities that may cause long-term damage to her body, like weightlifting.
  • Any health problems that she has, e.g. if Naomi has joint problems she may be more likely to choose swimming, as it would put less pressure on the joints than weight-bearing exercise.
  • Any disabilities that Naomi has, e.g. if her local sports centre does not have accessible facilities for certain sports, this will affect which activities she can take part in.
  • Her personality, e.g. if Naomi is an extrovert, she may be more likely to enjoy taking part in fast team sports, like hockey. But if she is an introvert, she is more likely to want to do individual activities that require precision and concentration, like archery.

 This is a level marked question — the number of marks you get will depend on what points you made, <u>and</u> how well you explained and organised them. The maximum mark for this question is 8 marks.
 You get 2 marks for naming two factors.
 You get 4 marks for giving at least two factors, with brief relevant examples showing how each factor might affect Naomi's participation.
 You get 8 marks for a well written and organised answer, giving at least three factors, with relevant and well developed examples.

2 (a) Naomi might e.g. enjoy coaching the team / make some new friends / improve her leadership skills / improve her knowledge of the game / make contacts that help her to get more involved in sport / improve her future job prospects *(1 mark each for any two benefits)*.

 (b) Knock-out competitions are played in rounds *(1 mark)*. Each team play one game per round *(1 mark)*. The team that wins each game goes through to the next round (the team that loses is out of the competition) *(1 mark)*.

 (c) Your answer should include some of the following points:

  • She could set the players a task to perform, e.g. dribbling a ball in and out of a set of cones, and use the results to explain to them how well they completed the task, e.g. by telling them how fast they did it.
  • This will help the players to work out their strengths and weaknesses, and develop an action plan to improve their performance.
  • She could set goals to help focus the players on their training.
  • Good feedback may also help to motivate players to work hard and improve their performance.
  • Naomi could give a player verbal guidance, e.g. she could watch them perform a skill, and explain what they did well and what they did wrong.
  • Then the players will know which parts of the skill they need to practice, so they can perform the skill better next time.
  • Naomi could give the players visual guidance, e.g. she could give them a demonstration of how to perform a skill correctly / show them videos of themselves performing a certain skill.
  • Naomi could give the players manual guidance, e.g. to teach a particular type of kick she could hold a player's lower leg and guide it through the correct motion.
  • Then the players will know how to perform the skill correctly, so they can practice it and improve their own performance of that skill.
  • Naomi could also give the players visual or verbal guidance when they are playing, e.g. she could shout or signal to them to remind them of where they should be on the pitch, or when to pass the ball.
  • This will help the players to improve their gameplay during matches.
  (1 mark for each point, up to a maximum of 8 marks)

 (d) Your answer should include some of the following points:
  • The team gets money from the sponsor to spend on things like new kit/clothing and equipment.
  • If the team wants to enter competitions they may have their travel and/or entry fees paid for them by the sponsor.
  • The team may get money from the sponsor to spend on improving their training facilities/ground.
  • Having their logo/name, e.g. on the team's kit, is a form of advertising. This will raise the profile of their business locally, and possibly lead to increased sales.
  • Sponsoring a local sports team may improve the company's public image in the local area.
  • If the team does well in any competitions, the sponsor will be associated with their success, improving the company's image.
  • The business may not have to pay tax on the money that they spend sponsoring the team.
  (6 marks for any six points)

 (e) Your answer should include some of the following points:
  • Naomi should do a risk assessment to make sure she has minimised any potential risks, and that the activities she has planned are as safe as possible for everyone taking part.
  • She should make sure that any new players are fit to take part, e.g. by doing the appropriate fitness tests with them/checking that their doctor has said they are fit to play/making them fill in a PAR-Q.
  • She should make sure people who are injured/ill do not take part in training — they may make their injuries worse, and are more likely to cause injuries to others.
  • Before the training session starts, Naomi should check the playing area for possible dangers, e.g. wet grass, litter, holes in the playing surface.
  • Naomi should check that any equipment the children will be using is safe, e.g. she should check that goalposts are in good condition and properly weighted and anchored.
  • She should make sure that the children are wearing suitable clothing/footwear before allowing them to take part in training, e.g. when playing outside they should be wearing studded boots.
  • Naomi should make sure that before starting any physical activity all of the players have completed a suitable warm-up.
  • Naomi should check that everyone knows the rules for all activities done in training sessions. She should make sure that the children follow these rules, and discipline anyone who breaks them.
  • Naomi should make sure that children of similar skill level and strength are playing against each other.
  • Naomi should make sure that the children cool-down properly at the end of training sessions to prevent stiffness/soreness and future injuries.
  • If the children need to lift or carry any equipment during the training session, Naomi should check that they are using the correct technique.

 This is a level marked question — the number of marks you get will depend on what points you made, <u>and</u> how well you explained and organised them. The maximum mark for this question is 7 marks.
 You get 3 marks for making three simple relevant points.
 You get 5 marks for making at least three relevant points, some of which are developed. You get 7 marks for a well written and organised answer, making at least four relevant and well developed points.

Index

Index

Make sure you're not missing out on another superb CGP revision book that might just save your life...

...order your **free** catalogue today.

CGP customer service is second to none

We work very hard to despatch all orders the **same day** we receive them, and our success rate is currently 99.9%. We send all orders by **overnight courier** or **First Class** post.
If you ring us today you should get your catalogue or book tomorrow. Irresistible, surely?

- Phone: 0870 750 1252   (Mon-Fri, 8.30am to 5.30pm)
- Fax: 0870 750 1292
- e-mail: orders@cgpbooks.co.uk
- Post: CGP, Kirkby-in-Furness, Cumbria, LA17 7WZ
- Website: www.cgpbooks.co.uk

...or you can ask at any good bookshop.